(Mis)adventures of a
Wishful Thinker

Sallie H. Weissinger

SHE WRITES PRESS

Published 2021
Printed in the United States of America
Print ISBN: 978-1-64742-315-5
E-ISBN: 978-1-64742-316-2
Library of Congress Control Number: 2021910754

For information, address:
She Writes Press
1569 Solano Ave #546
Berkeley, CA 94707

She Writes Press is a division of SparkPoint Studio, LLC.

Names and identifying characteristics have been changed to protect the privacy of certain individuals.

PRAISE FOR *YES, AGAIN*

"Sallie Weissinger celebrates her seventy-fifth birthday in *Yes, Again* by taking the reader on a tour of her big heart and where that heart has taken her. This glorious story of a life lived in love is the perfect read because it's hilarious, honest, and full of hope. We are all lovers, or we wish we were, and Sallie shows us how: never give up, occasionally give in, and don't stop believing. Brava!"

—Adriana Trigiani, best-selling author of *Tony's Wife*

"After reading Sallie's soulful book, I would have to say this gifted writer got the love she wanted the old-fashioned way . . . she earned it!"

—Lacy J. Dalton, singer and songwriter

"This captivating memoir of not giving up through profound losses and leaning into the promise of good things to come swelled my heart. With a chuckle and grit, Weissinger writes of her risky quest to find a new life and partner to love. Her vast and interesting life experiences make for intriguing reading. Pick up this book and see how she finds joy and delight!"

—Marilee Eaves, author of *Singing Out Loud*

To Bart,

who never met a lemon he didn't like

CONTENTS

1

"LOVE WILL FIND A WAY"

(Sam Cooke version)

For the record, I've never considered myself middle-aged. I didn't even think getting older was a possibility until the AARP publications started arriving. Little did I know they would arrive so soon and in such quantity that it would make it difficult to open or close my mailbox. Some people think AARP notifications are a sign one is approaching senior-hood, but I won't call myself a senior until I stop dancing to "Johnny B. Goode" and "Great Balls of Fire" as I did when I was fifteen with hips swiveling and booty shaking. And I won't stop dancing while there's the music of Chuck Berry and Jerry Lee Lewis to swivel and shake to.

Even at seventy-two, I still felt youngish. I'd been lonely for a long time, having lost my husband to esophageal cancer when I was fifty-seven, and I wanted to start looking for someone. But what was I looking for? Husband, companion, buddy?

I once read that "people yearn for three things in life: work they love, a person to love, and something to look forward to." It's a paraphrase of a quote by Tom Bodett, an American author, voice actor, and radio host who's appeared on NPR's *All Things Considered* and *Wait Wait Don't Tell Me*. That quote seemed particularly relevant to my situation at the time. I had found work I loved; now retired, my regimen of rich social activities, coursework, and volunteer work had replaced the professional satisfaction I experienced during the years I, briefcase in hand, caught the 5:52 a.m. BART into San Francisco five days a week. I felt good about my progress in Bodett's #1 work category. But #2, someone to love, had not materialized, and that had a definite effect on #3, something to look forward to.

I had used social media before to meet potential matches, but that was back when social media meant newspapers and magazines. In 1978, I had no time to meet a man. I was divorced and barely managing to raise an eight-year-old daughter, Heather. Even with a master's in Spanish and French Literature and seven years of experience, I'd been unable to find a high school or community college teaching job. So I'd worked at a stock brokerage, an audio visual rental company, and, worst of all, as a bilingual secretary at an elegantly appointed European bank, where my German boss would call me into his office when I finished typing a letter and hold it up to the light, examining the sheet of paper carefully to see if I'd used Correcto-Type to cover up a typo. I never did, but I would have if I'd thought it would have escaped his eagle eye. Once, he revealed his Nazi leanings when he confided to me, "Fräulein Weissinger, we know Hitler was right, *ja*?" Another time he chased me around the desk in his closed office, rubbing both hands on my breasts. I ran out of his office and sat at my desk, sobbing, knowing I had to quit. But I couldn't support Heather if I did. I started looking for another job.

Fortunately, I landed a position as a vocational rehabilitation counselor for an insurance company, with a client load of twenty to twenty-five industrial workers injured on the job, scattered over the 180 miles from Salinas to Sacramento. Hired because I was fluent in Spanish, my mandate was to help my clients get back to work. This job was a godsend.

In addition to a healthier and more challenging work environment, the new job provided increased income, although every month I worried about billing enough hours to cover the rent, food, and Heather's education and extended day care. But the job gave me the opportunity to speak the language I had worked hard to master; the field was challenging, most of my clients were motivated, and I was my own boss. It also gave me more time to be with my daughter. Sometimes I could spend whole afternoons with her; then, after she went to bed, I'd sit at the kitchen table, writing reports in those pre-home computer days. Attempting to be a full-time breadwinner and mother was a juggling act, but it was getting easier. What it didn't leave time for, however, was finding a life partner and soul mate.

When I lamented my solo status to my former apartment manager, longtime friend, and to this day brother-equivalent, Russ, he suggested, "Why not try the *Bay Guardian*?" The widely distributed and wildly popular *Guardian* was a free newspaper covering left-leaning politics, cultural events, and, of course (being San Francisco-based), drugs and sex with scandalous articles designed to shock all but the most liberal readers. (The paper also printed a much-coveted annual nude beach issue.) To my Southern belle way of thinking, the paper overstepped the bounds of propriety by leaps and bounds.

"Russ," I told him, "the *Guardian* is too weird. It's tacky. That's what losers do. I can't do that."

"Sallie, you're wrong. I've met impressive women through the personals; they're not losers or pathetic or even close to that," Russ chided me.

Ultimately I gave in. I picked up three weekly issues of the newspaper and marked a total of twenty personals ads with a red pen. I sent fourteen letters to the *Guardian* PO boxes listed. Eight of the fourteen men responded to me, and I met five of them. The brief coffee dates convinced me the men doing the personals weren't psychopaths. I enjoyed meeting them, even if I wasn't finding "him." To prepare how to present myself in my ad, I studied how other women described themselves—sensuous, sensual, highly imaginative, erotically oriented, skilled in amorous techniques, and curvaceous in body—and then went in a different direction, keeping the text as short as I could to minimize the cost:

> Share the good things. Attractive, sensitive, professional W/F, 34, seeks male kindred soul, someone bright, serious, fun, strong, gentle. Guardian Box 12-51-E.

I ran the ad twice at a cost of around forty dollars. Maybe forty-five.

Over the next few weeks, I received and sorted sixty responses into three piles: twelve YESes, forty NOs, and eight MAYBEs. The NOs were easiest to categorize. I instantly rejected letters from:

- numerous older men who specifically sought younger women,
- a man and his wife looking for a threesome,

- a twenty-year-old college student who was hoping for "an experienced, older woman for hot tubbing and smoking weed while watching the sun set over the Golden Gate," and
- two prisoners at San Quentin who wanted me to visit them on weekends.

The only NO that I answered was an articulate, sensitive man who wrote me that his wife had advanced multiple sclerosis, and he hoped to find a sexual relationship and close friendship. He did not want to mislead me: he loved his wife and would stay with her until she passed away. Without mentioning my last name or address, I wrote, saying I sympathized with his situation and wished him the best in his search.

I met every one of the twelve men in the YES group for coffee in Berkeley, Oakland, or San Francisco. They were engaging, intelligent, and accomplished. I met the conductor of a local Bay Area symphony chorus; a novelist working part-time as a postman and getting his master's in English; a UC Berkeley professor of history; and Tim, a manager at Xerox. (I've changed the names and some details of the men I discuss in this book.)

Tim's ex-wife, Joan, had responded to my ad on her ex-husband's behalf without his knowledge. He was still her best friend, but their relatively short marriage hadn't worked out. She said more than enough about him—brainy, kind, hardworking, great sense of humor, outdoorsy and fit, adventurous—to intrigue me. She gave me his office phone number. It took a while to get my nerve up, but I finally phoned him, dialing very slowly. When he answered, I stammered uncomfortably, "Hi, Tim . . . um . . . my name is Sallie and I know you aren't expecting my call, but . . . Joan responded to my personals ad in the *Bay Guardian*. She thinks you and I might have a lot in common."

The next thing he said after "Hello" was, "Hey, guys, can we finish this meeting in a little while?" He sounded puzzled.

"Go on," Tim said after he had his office to himself. I gulped and continued, "Joan says you're athletic and outdoorsy, and so am I. And you like to read and travel. Er . . . would you like to meet for coffee sometime?"

Flummoxed, he agreed to a Saturday afternoon encounter. I liked him on sight—he was the only one of the dozen men in the YES category who made my stomach do flip-flops. Two or three years older than I was, Tim was handsome with medium-length brown hair and brownish-green eyes. He was dressed a notch below preppy casual, without sinking into Berkeley shaggy: clean jeans and a nicely ironed wine-colored shirt, with long sleeves rolled up to his mid-forearms. I recognized him first and introduced myself. "Hi, Tim, thanks for meeting me. I know it's a little weird for you."

"Yep," he agreed, straining to smile.

We sat down and talked over coffee for forty-five minutes. The conversation was pleasant but strained, with talk centering mostly on his work and mine. We weren't connecting, and I knew it but couldn't do anything to change the dynamic. I tried to get him to talk more about personal things—he'd briefly mentioned bike rides and hikes he'd taken—but I had minimal luck. I was disappointed when he didn't call after our awkward get-together. But I could tell he wasn't ready to pursue a relationship. He was, I assumed, still in love with his ex-wife and might have suspected she'd contacted me to assuage her guilt at choosing to end the marriage.

At that point, I had met all the YESes and my plan was to dump the MAYBEs into the NO pile and repeat my ad. I'd enjoyed my adventure and felt jazzed, confident I'd find the ideal man within a reasonable time. But first I'd make my profile text a little longer and a little zingier. I was determined not to worry about what it would cost to run it for another two weeks. I'd go for the big bucks: sixty dollars. Maybe seventy-five!

But there was a hitch. One MAYBE guy, Matt, had included a photo of himself on a beach with his Australian shepherd, along with a self-addressed stamped envelope. He requested the photo back because it was the only one he had of his beloved dog, Pirate, now living with his ex-wife and four daughters. I had decided not to meet him because his response struck me as glib and self-important. Still, I had to return the photo. But the price of mailing a letter had gone up, and I needed to add a two-cent stamp. Finally, after two weeks of not getting to the post office, I figured it was easier just to meet him.

Matt and I met at Ortman's Ice Cream and Sandwich Parlor. With its white walls, old-fashioned counter with cheerful red stools, and charming small white wrought iron tables and chairs, Ortman's was the equivalent of a neighborhood bar for families with small kids. It was my daughter's and my favorite place to go—our warm spot, our home away from home. Unwilling to primp up for a MAYBE guy, I wore blue jeans, a blue work shirt, and a navy blue parka. The most I'd done to prepare for our meeting was to comb my hair, which back then was a frizzy perm.

I was seated at a small round table for two when Matt entered and walked toward me, making his way between the tables of animated customers. He was wearing a long-sleeved, red-checked shirt, a brown leather vest, jeans, brown boots, and a soft gray wool Scottish-style fishing hat. "Jaunty" was the word that came to mind as he approached me with a self-confident, lively stride. Jaunty. I recall thinking to myself, "He's attractive. But what's with the hat?"

We introduced ourselves, and he sat down, leaning forward with his arms on the table. We fell into easy conversation. It didn't take any prodding to get him to talk. And Matt asked me questions, listened to my responses, then asked more questions. "You're divorced, right? Why did you get divorced?" I recounted the short version of my failed marriage: how both Daniel and I were military brats. "We went to ninth grade together in Tokyo, and he told me then he was going to marry me. I didn't believe him, but that's what happened. We wrote each other for eight years, then met again when I was in graduate school at Berkeley and he was in advanced infantry training at Fort Ord." I explained that, at twenty, Daniel and I had a lot in common; at twenty-nine, I'd changed from being the girl he knew to a woman he didn't. "I wasn't willing to be a dutiful military wife, as both our mothers had been. Their husbands were their careers."

I told Matt that Daniel had volunteered for Vietnam over my protests. "Besides, I wanted a shared relationship, with both of us supporting the family financially, both of us sharing child care, and both of us helping out at home. Daniel's world view didn't include helping with the dishes, running a load of laundry, or making himself a sandwich. I gave him six months' notice to shape up or I would ship out. He didn't."

Matt nodded for me to go on. "But why leave Louisiana?"

"I came to California," I continued, "because my mother was upset at my decision to leave my marriage. She said Daniel hadn't 'beaten me, run around with other women, gambled, or turned into an alcoholic or drug addict,'" the only four reasons that, to her, would justify a woman's leaving her marriage. "I couldn't stay in New Orleans and listen to more of that. I had to leave." I sensed that this man was not only listening to me, but getting me as a person.

While Matt was asking me questions, I was squeezing in my own questions, to learn everything I could about this intriguing man.

"You've asked why I left. Now it's my turn: why did you and your wife get divorced?"

With a pained look in his eyes, he confided, "I waited way too long. I should have called it quits after Jane started drinking seven years into the marriage. But by then we'd had three girls, and I couldn't leave them. And no judge would give the children to their father unless the mother simply couldn't function at all. Believe me—I checked around, but I didn't want to ask them to testify against their mother. That would have been the only way."

He went on to tell me he stayed seven more years, and her drinking got worse and worse. They fought openly, in front of the (now four) kids. As a trial attorney, he'd argue cases during the day, come home, and argue with Jane during the evening and into the night. A few years before we met, with his wife complaining about the reduced income, he'd left his downtown San Francisco firm for a job with the state of California. "Private practice was bringing out my worst qualities. I considered myself a 'paid gladiator' and didn't like who I was becoming." As a judicial educator, he was relieved, writing bench guides for new judges and coordinating programs in which experienced judges trained incoming judges. Matt and his wife separated, and he moved to an unfurnished studio apartment in Berkeley, where he slept in a sleeping bag on the floor, while maintaining his family in their house in affluent Marin County.

By this point in our conversation, I couldn't swallow any more of my root beer float. I was swooning. This MAYBE candidate wasn't the way he'd seemed in his letter. Glib? Not at all. He was revealing his feelings and was eager to learn about me. The longer we talked, the more there was to talk about. We leaned increasingly closer to one another, unaware of the customers around us entering, ordering, sipping, eating, paying, leaving. The anticipated hour to hand over a snapshot turned into an animated hour and a half of exchanging intimate confidences. Strangely enough, it didn't seem unusual to have spoken so openly with someone I wouldn't have recognized without his photo in my hand. Now he knew more about me than my coworkers or friends in California did. We had discussed how we had recrafted our lives by resolving work miseries, overcoming marital disappointments, and nurturing our daughters. Our miseries and disappointments had led us serendipitously to this special place, on this magical evening. Here we were, sitting across from each other in an ice cream parlor, talking as if we had known each other forever.

By the time we realized it was time to get up from the table, Ortman's was nearly empty. We hadn't noticed how quiet the store had become; our voices were the only sounds to be heard. Matt had long since finished his iced tea and polished off my root beer float. Reluctant to say good-bye, we stood in front of the ice cream parlor and shook hands for longer than a handshake should take. I invited Matt to dinner at my house the next week, and he accepted. "I'd like that. A lot." I remember hoping he'd kiss me on the cheek, but he didn't. When I got home, I raced to my *Guardian* file and reread his letter. I shook my head. "What was I thinking? He's better than all the YESes. Where's glib? Where's self-important?" Something promising had definitely happened, but I wouldn't prematurely count chickens. Still, with more than a few butterflies flying around in my stomach, I shelved my plans to revise my personals ad for the time being.

Matt insisted on bringing some of the food to our dinner. "I'll bring the main dish and dessert. I'm expanding my limited culinary repertoire, one recipe at a time," he said, laughing. "I'm tired of ramen and scrambled eggs."

He showed up the following Thursday at the appointed six thirty. Both of us were smiling as I opened the door. He handed me a spinach frittata and a cheesecake, both made from scratch, along with a bottle of red wine. Given that my ex-husband had been unwilling to learn to use a can opener, I was pleased Matt was boisterously invading so-called women's territory with a masculine flourish. My heart skipped a few clichéd beats. "Come in. Your frittata is beautiful," I said, trying to hide my nervousness.

We sat at the kitchen table and talked as easily as before. Our conversation continued without interruption, since Heather had been invited to spend the night with a school friend. We ate the frittata and the salad and drank a second glass of wine. Once again, I had trouble swallowing my food, but the wine went down easily.

Matt had turned on the radio to a channel with Big Band music. After finishing his last bite of frittata, he stood up, took my hand, lifted me from my chair, and put his arm around my waist. "Let's dance," he said. Frank Sinatra sang "These Foolish Things" and then "It's not the pale moon that excites me, that thrills and delights me. Oh, no, it's just the nearness of you." The music was slow and romantic, and we both sang the lyrics word for word. He had a firm grasp on my back, and I followed easily. Everything was Hollywood dreamy, including when he said, "You follow well and are light on your feet." Of course I was light on my feet—I was levitating. And when he added, "I love how your body feels against mine," it didn't sound smarmy or practiced. It just felt like the truth.

We had cheesecake for breakfast the next morning.

2

"OVER THE RAINBOW"

(Israel [IZ] Kamakawiwo'ole version)

Those first encounters led to a twenty-four-year relationship. Matt and I, as a girlfriend said, "were welded at the hip." Matt helped me raise Heather, and I became a favorite aunt to his daughters. He died in early 2002 at age sixty-nine.

It took a year after his death before I'd begun to recover somewhat from days and nights of crying. As much as I missed him, I had "ants in my pants," as my mother would say about my lifelong tendency to stay busy, to keep going and doing. I hoped to find a congenial person to spend time with when my girlfriends were with their mates—someone who wanted to go to a movie, take a hike, make dinner, sip wine. Or just talk. Small steps would be fine. And so I announced I was going to try my luck with the new and improved version of the personals: online dating.

I found it embarrassing and depressing to be shopping for love, but gently aging swains were not falling at my feet at the grocery store or gas station. Moving my wedding band to the ring finger on my right hand, I forged ahead. (Sweet Pea said, "You did this at thirty-four and it worked out. You can do it at fifty-eight." Steve disagreed, "This could take a really long time.")

Allow me to introduce Sweet Pea and Steve, the positive and negative voices in my head. They pop up on occasion, often at the same time. We all have those interior points of view that buoy us or belittle us, encourage us to do right or wrong, to be bold or boring. At least I hope I'm not the only one who hears at times from her zanier self and at other times from her practical alter ego. Sweet Pea is the nickname I gave to my dazzling mother, and Steve is named for my military dad, who had a tendency to criticize. They aren't my parents, but they are the essence of them.

I opened accounts with match.com and OkCupid, the two online personals sites I'd heard the most about. I drafted, edited, and painstakingly reedited my profile narrative and submitted a few photos. Again rejecting the sexy, heavy-on-makeup look, I chose photos that showed me as slim, natural looking, and okay-pretty, not hot-beautiful. Other than a once-a-day application of a muted color of lipstick, I don't use cosmetics. Even back in college, when my girlfriends wanted me to slather myself with mascara, eyeliner, and foundation, I balked at trying to look artificially provocative, and I always seemed to smear the mascara. Besides, I remembered what Matt told me our first month together. "I'm glad you don't use war paint. You don't need it, and it's dumb and expensive."

On the online dating sites, I examined men's postings carefully, starting with their checklist classifications: unmarried heterosexuals (preferably widowed or divorced as opposed to never married and probably unable to make a commitment), living within a reasonable geographic area (ideally not more than fifty to seventy-five miles), college graduates, age range of fifty-five to sixty-five. I was open to agnostics, atheists, Jews, Buddhists, and Christians, as long as their beliefs might coexist with my brand of agnostic secular humanism. I skipped over those who self-identified as smokers and political conservatives. Also barred from consideration, as in the *Bay Guardian* days, were men who sought cutting-edge sexual adventure, preferred polyamorous thrills, or revealed they were married but wanted a fling.

Two additional attributes were deal breakers. First, I wasn't interested in an out-of-shape, overweight man. **(Steve: "I thought you weren't supposed to judge a book by its cover." Sweet Pea: "So what if she's a snob about weight? She isn't asking for a senior triathlete, just someone who takes pride in his appearance.")** The categories in the profiles were athletic, slim, about average, and stout. It became dismayingly clear that men checked "about average" when even their best photos showed them as stout and evidently gym-averse.

I'm fussy about weight because I was a chubby size fourteen in my last two years of high school and into my early twenties. Back then it was called being "pleasingly plump," but I saw nothing pleasing about the extra twenty pounds I was carrying. My sister called me "Sal, Sal, the Metrecal Gal" because I was dieting on Metrecal's liquid calories instead of the spaghetti, French fries, and brownies I craved. My first husband, Daniel, a fitness buff, often asked me, "Do you really need to eat that?" as I buttered a roll or took a second helping of rice at a dinner party. Several times he said, both before and during our marriage, "I love you, but would love you more if you lost weight." I have continued to be sensitive about weight issues, and, as I've aged, been sure to keep exercising—jogging (before my knees started hurting), brisk walking at least four miles a day now, and going to the gym. Because I've worked hard to maintain a sensible weight, I expect the man to be equally disciplined.

Second, if a man said he out-and-out disliked pets, that was a no-go.

The most revealing thing about a potential match was his narrative. I wanted to read in his own words who he was as a person, a mate, a parent. What moved his heart? How did he spend his time? What did he think about? Read, watch, listen to? What did he miss having in his life? Women may go overboard, telling more than enough (my approach), but men often skipped this section entirely or provided disappointingly skimpy information. I was turned off by spelling and grammar mistakes a junior high school student shouldn't make. I moved on quickly if I read "I like to go out to eat and please my pallet." "Life has it's ups and downs, but I'm a servivor." "Seek open-minded woman with liberal sense of hummer." And "I am adventurious, enegertic, love to please my patner. I have many blessings and want to share them with the right women." Women—plural? Was this yet another spelling error or a push for polyamory? In either case, no thanks.

I looked to see what Mr. Potential Partner considered a good time. If he wanted "to sit on the couch with a sexy lady and drink margaritas while we watch Sunday afternoon football," I moved on to a different profile. Nor did I seek a coffee offer with the guy who enjoyed "cleaning my muscle car and doing yard work." I liked the photo of an attractive blue-eyed man with his enticingly shaggy brown-and-white dog but wasn't drawn to his story: "I am spending my retirement playing around with my '57

Chevy. It would be good to have a nice lady to take to car shows and kick back with a glass of wine. I quit smoking eight months ago, quit drinking two years ago. Only thing left is fast cars and fast women." He put a smiley face after the "fast women" comment. But I didn't understand how he'd quit drinking two years earlier and yet was up for a good glass of wine. It didn't matter—I wasn't up for the car shows. More appealing—though not sufficiently—were the attractive, outdoorsy men who wanted to ride motorcycles or drive their RVs across the country, sail to Hawaii, or fish in the Caribbean. I hoped they'd find the perfect companions to share their ride, but none of them would be me.

The images of a lot of the men showed we had nothing in common. More than a few were wrapped in the American flag or wore a shirt or jacket with a flag theme; some wore baseball caps with their military squadron emblem embroidered on the bill or were dressed in their Vietnam-era uniforms with a splash of medals. It wasn't so much that I was antiwar back in the sixties (although I was); it was that the 'Nam look said to me that here was someone stuck in the past. Even less attractive were those sporting partial- and full-arm tattoos, not to mention one guy with a tat linking his eyebrows. Not for me were the multi-pierced men with bandannas crowning their shoulder-length hair; bearded Santa Claus types wearing John Deere caps and drinking beer; or Hells Angels wannabes in black leather-fringed jackets and pants, sitting on motorcycles. Also discounted were the dude with obviously dyed, coal-black Dracula-style hair, a black it had never been in his twenties; the bare-chested, bicep-flexing jock in shorts, proud of his pectorals and six-pack abs; and the one whose selfies made him look like a wanted criminal on FBI posters.

I did find men with qualities I sought, although fewer than I'd hoped: those with an intellectual orientation and professional work background; ones who'd been in love and sought a friend, not a hot babe; some who mentioned the importance of holding family close. I looked to see if a man my age was fine with a woman my age—many of them wanted women ten to fifteen years younger—and I wasn't going to fib about how old I was. And I cast a sharp eye to see if he described himself as fit. **(Steve: "Wow, she's really hung up on this." Sweet Pea: "Nothing wrong with having standards.")** I looked for someone who mentioned rewarding volunteer and community activities. If he stated a desire to travel with a co-adventurer, that was a huge plus. I searched for images showing him with a pet at his side, hiking in mountains near and far, eating in an outdoor café with his grandchildren, or hanging out in the backyard with friends and family. What Matt would have called a mensch.

I sent messages to those whose checklists, narratives, and photos boded well. "You've caught my eye," I told them. If I liked their smiles or lively eyes or something else noteworthy in their photos (hiking! yay! cooking! a garden! dogs! cats!), I mentioned it. I edited my messages to come across as more upbeat and optimistic than I often felt. Still, each time I clicked the SEND button, I let my heart surge at the possibility of resuming a colorful life.

I received responses from too few of those to whom I sent messages. Messages came in slowly, some from seekers in their sixties, but many from men in their seventies and eighties, older men I had considered outside my preferred age pool. Men around my age, if they responded, often wrote they wanted mates in their late thirties to early fifties—I was too old at fifty-eight for a man in the sixty-to-sixty-five-year bracket? My sister, stepdaughters, and friends continued to encourage me to seek a younger man, saying, "People your age can't keep up with you. You have the energy and looks of a woman in her forties." I hoped that was true. Still, the age thing was an unavoidable reality. I emailed the small group of appropriate, age-desirable men who'd either responded affirmatively to my e-contact or who'd contacted me straight off. I thanked the others who didn't appear to be a match and wished them well in their search. That is a mantra of mine: "We are all seekers. Wish everyone well."

Meeting guys began with exchanging first names and cell phone numbers and agreeing to talk on the phone. I would try to sound interested and enthusiastic, but not anxious or needy. Upbeat but not excessively chipper. Smart but not geeky. Friendly without being too chatty.

As much as I wanted to meet people, it annoyed me to gussy myself up for the meetings. My daily look is REI/L.L. Bean: Levi's jeans and a T-shirt or work shirt, with a fleece jacket on chilly days. If I were meeting someone who was coming from work or who had invited me to meet at an upscale location, I upped the ante: black slacks, a long-sleeved top with a bright scarf, and flats in lieu of walking shoes. I'd check myself in the mirror before leaving the house and ask, "Do I look okay? Is my outfit tight enough to be attractive but not too revealing? Casual but not grubby? Did I put on enough lipstick or too much?"

Me worrying about makeup? As I concluded last-minute prepping and primping, I'd shake my head at the mirror, the human sandwich board flashing "ALONE AND LONELY." Then I'd look one final time, give myself the nothing-ventured, nothing-gained pep talk, and pet whichever of my two dogs or two cats was nearby. With purse, iPhone, and car keys in hand, I'd head for the door. (Steve: "Why bother? It's not going to work." Sweet Pea: "This could be THE person. This could be the MAYBE who becomes a YES. Remember MATT!") Anyway, it was good practice. I thought of myself as a patient with a broken leg, in need of physical therapy. I would keep doing my exercises.

The hardest exercise was to practice using "I" in conversation, substituting it for the entrenched "we." It was more than a linguistic challenge. It meant rejiggering my identity, rewiring my heart and my mind, wiping away the past to start with a clean slate.

By and large, the men I met were nice and presentable. Usually nothing was wrong, but nothing was right either. They were my "arms-legs-English" coffee dates: the guys had two arms, two legs, and spoke English. It was pleasant enough, but nothing I wanted to pursue. A fair number of guys had lied about their ages or had posted photos that bore little resemblance to their current appearance. At times I could barely contain my fury. I wanted to call them out: "How many years ago was your photo taken? Why would you do that?" Instead, I swallowed my annoyance, kept chatting, checked to see when forty-five minutes were up and I could leave gracefully. After a few of these experiences, I revised my mantra: "We are all seekers. Wish everyone well, even the flagrant liars."

The first year I averaged two or three coffee meetings a month in the East Bay and San Francisco—my profile was new on the sites, and rookies get contacted. After my newcomer status ended, meetings decreased to one or at most two a month.

I had spells of weeks and months when I didn't reach out to anyone. I sent emails to those who contacted me, but with whom I felt nothing in common, telling them I'd met someone and wishing them good luck. But every so often a message, photo, or profile suggested I might be one cup of coffee away from finding "him"—or "HIM"—the irresistibly brainy, animal-loving swashbuckler I hankered for. Things looked even more promising when an email led to an upbeat phone call that resulted in an agreement to meet in person. Then the sliver of hope turned into a golden ray of sunshine. This one was going to be different.

One man in particular sounded like a possibility. Doug had an MA in English from Berkeley and taught in community college. His profile said he liked to read and go to the theater. But he showed up for coffee in a torn, dirt-encrusted, mustard-colored sweatshirt and jeans that screamed to be washed. The photo he'd posted was at least ten years old.

"I've only got an hour or so till I have to get back."

I was relieved he was facing a time limit. I asked where "back" was.

"I'm painting some apartments and having trouble patching the walls. The paint's not covering, and I've gotta talk to the paint store guys before they close, to see what they suggest." As we talked, it became clear he hadn't taught for over twenty years, and even then it had been part-time; now he was a handyman for a Berkeley landlord. The conversation limped along until I reminded him about his pressing paint problems.

Other encounters left me feeling similarly disappointed. After our introductory greetings, one coffee date, a tax attorney from Alameda, went on interminably about why he preferred the Oakland Raiders to the San Francisco 49ers. He and I wouldn't be going out for a second cup of coffee, much less to a tailgate party at the Oakland Coliseum.

In time I stopped being surprised and dismayed that eighteen out of twenty coffee companions asked zero questions about me. It was clear they preferred to talk about themselves. Often as we said good-bye, they'd tell me they'd enjoyed our talk and asked to meet again. But we hadn't talked. They had talked, and I had listened.

Health started to play an increasingly larger role in these coffee encounters. Impaired mobility, heart operations, lists of medications, and details of aches and pains were frequent subjects for first meetings. One time I got to the agreed-upon coffee shop first and was sipping a cappuccino when my prospect walked in. He introduced himself, placed an inflatable ring on the chair next to me, and sat down gingerly. "I need this donut cushion because of my hemorrhoids," he said. "I had an operation last week." (Steve: "Good god, not hemorrhoids! What kind of idiots are you meeting?") I was at a loss for a response. I wondered whether I should ask him how his prostate was. (Sweet Pea: "Go ahead. I want to hear this.")

More than occasionally over ten years, I considered stopping the search. I guess I stayed the course because of a combination of hard-wired obstinacy and innate optimism. And there was one other component—I equated giving up with accepting death, the death of hope for change.

A few introductory coffee encounters turned into short-term dating. I went out with at least ten men for one to two months, following our perfunctory first cups of coffee. I wanted to see if, given time and opportunity, something might develop with the occasional man who stood out from the field of forgettable ones.

I dated an insect biologist from Berkeley, who was using fruit fly mutants to develop a genetic model of epilepsy and assessing if his experiments could be applied to humans. An IT consultant from San Francisco and I went bicycling along the ocean, and he cooked me dinner. With them, and others, I enjoyed myself, but waited—and I imagine they did too—for the recognizable click that chemistry and good fortune can generate. That didn't happen.

And then two men caught my attention. The first was Dwight, a retired computer systems analyst and artist from

Chicago. He'd relocated to be near his daughter and grandson in the Bay Area, where he set up a studio in his apartment. I admired his bold brush strokes and his use of brilliant saturated colors in his oil paintings, which tended toward large landscapes.

Dwight was sweet and affectionate, but not as bold and colorful a man as he was a painter. He wanted me to decide which movie to go to. He wasn't sure whether he should rent the apartment with the larger kitchen or the larger bedroom. He wanted to know if I thought he should sell his condo back in Illinois or rent it out short- or long-term. I was impatient with his inability to make a decision. He leaned on me too much. I was in no position to make decisions regarding his living situation—I just knew I wasn't going to invite him to live in my house. We stopped dating after three months.

The second man, Adam, was cultured, kind, and physically active. A retired internist, he had worked for the National Institutes of Health and the Veterans Administration. We loved many of the same things: cats, gardening, bike riding, music, books, plays, and movies. But he was a nut about cleaning his house. One Saturday afternoon I arrived at his house for our date to find him wearing an apron with two front pockets, each of which contained a spray bottle filled with a special formula. One bottle contained a pre-cleaning product and the other was for the second, final cleaning, administering the *coup de grace* to the few visible specks of dirt. Adam greeted me distractedly, asking me to wait two hours until he finished cleaning the kitchen and bathroom, after which we'd figure out our plans for the rest of the afternoon and evening. I was dismayed that he was more enthusiastic about his cleaning regimen than about our time together. His aging incontinent cat was another problem. There was a significant odor to the house that no amount of either cleaning product could neutralize. Our relationship sputtered out after four months. But, as with Dwight, it was a start.

I realize now that I was a flawed candidate for a relationship. Despite their faults, Dwight and Adam were more emotionally available than I was. I hadn't intended to mislead or take advantage of them. I couldn't have known at the time they would serve as my training wheels. They guided me along the bumpy road of mating territory at my clumsy pace as I grappled with seemingly minor issues I didn't know how to handle: Do I wait for him to open the car door for me? Will he be insulted if I want to pay my share of dinner? How do I keep from crying? These men, patient, gentle and kind, accepted my lack of grace, my dating klutziness, and my flood of tears when they said they wanted more from me. Even now, so many years later, I feel I owe them an apology.

3

"I STILL HAVEN'T FOUND WHAT I'M LOOKING FOR"

(U2)

In the midst of these going-nowhere online connections, I met Keith. I thought he was the gently aging, quirky person I'd been seeking. Part of me loved him and all of me loved parts of him. I loved his intellect, his sense of humor, his gentleness with his children and grandchildren, his affection for pets, and his sweetness. Initially, we didn't let the fact that we lived three hours apart get in our way. We spent extended weekends together, walking our dogs twice a day. We shopped for groceries and cooked. We traveled to New Zealand and Buenos Aires. For the first time I felt normal, not the emotional amputee I had been at times.

Keith loved sports and especially baseball—he'd been the star pitcher on both his high school and college teams. Every year he went with a group of his pals to the San Francisco Giants' spring training in Scottsdale; they bought the cheaper seats, out in the blistering Arizona sun. One year I went along, surprised to learn that, even in March, it was not unusual to be exposed to ninety-degree heat. I also learned that it is an accepted custom to sit in the pricier shaded areas until the rightful owners arrive and you have to give them their reserved seats. The first time we had to move, I hadn't known we weren't in the right seats. Keith and company, me included, went to a second shaded area. Twenty minutes later, we were evicted again. I was uncomfortable when Keith and his friends immediately headed for another row of vacant shaded seats and told him I didn't want to be thrown out a third time. "It's embarrassing to sit in a place we haven't paid for. It's just a matter of time until we'll be told to buzz off. Why don't we just go sit in the sun? That's what we paid for." He and his friends smiled at me with forbearance. "Sallie," Keith said gently, but in an amused tone, "this isn't the opera. This is baseball." The others nodded their heads in agreement. I went with them to the next set of unoccupied seats. I must have further confirmed my outsider status by reading a book instead of watching the practice.

His friends witnessed a more grievous lapse in my sports knowledge the following year. Every weekday Keith and his friends met at Duffy's, a sports bar, to watch any and every athletic event on the oversized television behind the bar. Keith typically had a vodka tonic or two, unless it was hot and he preferred a beer or two. One afternoon I joined him, a relative rarity on my part. I sat next to him, with his friends on both sides, and watched the two basketball teams chase the ball down one end of the court and up the other, as crowds on both sides applauded and booed at the bouncing, throwing, shuffling, catching, and dribbling. Even though I've never been enthusiastic about watching teams manipulating a ball on a grassy field, a wood floor, or a sandy beach, friends and family members have made sure I've watched my share of football, basketball, volleyball, and soccer. Given my past high school experience as a cheerleader and pep club president, I knew how basketball was played. And I knew from the ribbon running at the bottom of the screen that the teams were in the second quarter, eight minutes remained till half time, and the score was close. But I didn't understand and asked Keith, as quietly as I could, to clarify why the United Kingdom (listed as UK) was playing Uganda (UGA) on American TV. Keith's friends heard me. Keith explained patiently, "Sallie, this is a college game, and Kentucky is playing Georgia." The embarrassment I experienced at Duffy's outdid anything I'd felt at the Giants' spring training.

But this retired college professor wouldn't talk about anything deep or personal. Early in our relationship, I chastised Keith for not sharing his thoughts and feelings with me, for keeping to himself revelations about his childhood, his marriage and divorce, confidences about whatever touched him deeply. I asked in frustration, "Why don't you talk to me? Is Gary Cooper your role model? Randolph Scott?"—referring to the handsome Western hero actors, the embodiments of the tight-lipped cowboy figures of our preteen years. Without skipping a beat, Keith responded to me, "Ah likes to talk to mah horse."

A major concern was his heart problem, for which he'd been prescribed medication he didn't take, although I didn't know that at the time. What I did know was that he'd had at least three episodes during which he'd lost consciousness. Two of those times I'd been with him; I got him to a medical clinic the first time and to a hospital emergency room the second time. Both times he assured me that he would follow up with his primary care doctor, and I should not be concerned. After the emergency room visit, I insisted he tell his daughter about his medical issues. She had his power of attorney for health care and lived five minutes from his home.

"Sallie, I don't want to worry her. And, besides, my health is not your business." I was enraged and snapped, "Keith, if your health is none of my business, then you are none of my business." Grabbing my purse, my keys, and my dogs, I drove off. It hurt terribly that he wouldn't let me into his world to the extent that I wanted to inhabit it. I overrode his decision not to tell his daughter about what had happened. I couldn't bear the thought of her not being there should another medical emergency arise, since I evidently could not serve that role for him.

He called to apologize, but our patched-up relationship continued to go downhill. He didn't follow his doctor's orders to exercise. He drank more than I was comfortable with. With all the ways in which we hit it off, our differences in energy and communication styles were major obstacles for us both. He liked to sit and read and listen to music for hours on end. I liked to do that too, but not all the time. Keith could sit most of the day in his man cave of a den, ensconced in a green velvet chair I called his "bubba chair." But I wanted to walk, go hiking and biking, go to the gym, garden, and work on his house. The ants in my pants rarely slept. I worried that his idea of our life together would include "his" and "hers" bubba chairs.

One Saturday morning, I asked Keith if we could work for a few hours in his jungle of a backyard and then go to a movie. "Do you have an 'off' button?" he replied.

My irritated response slipped out before I could catch myself: "Do you have an 'on' button?"

In the end, our commuting back and forth stopped making sense. We broke up seven times over five or six years, each time without resolving the problems we'd had all along. The last time, we broke up for good. For months thereafter, many nights I reached for the phone at our traditional nine o'clock talking time, but I couldn't let myself call him, couldn't go back and break up again, not with someone I cared for so much. It was going to be one hundred percent or nothing.

Knowing I had come close, but not close enough, triggered serious soul-searching. I questioned whether I'd ever meet the right person. To what extent was I the problem—what was wrong with me? Were my expectations unreasonable? Was I looking for the single submicroscopic needle in a vast haystack and missing out on numerous acceptable larger needles in plain sight? (Steve: "Yes." Sweet Pea: "No.") But I had met Matt, hadn't I? If I'd found the so-called impossible once, I could find it again. With difficulty maybe, but it could happen.

I joined Our Time and Zoosk and dumped the other dating sites. I met two men I liked a lot. The one who made my heart beat the fastest was a widower from upstate New York named Brian. A retired senior IT director, he owned a condo near Berkeley, but his primary home was back East. Atypically, we bypassed the perfunctory coffee when he invited me to dinner for our first encounter. We met at an Italian restaurant in a hundred-year-old white Cape Cod-style Victorian building. Its romantic, down-home ambience, panoramic view of the Bay, and appetizing Italian food and wine list were a welcome replacement for a string of lackluster coffee shops and cafés.

We talked about hiking and traveling, two things we had in common. We'd both spent time in Europe and compared notes about our favorite areas in southern France. He'd been to Sicily; I was planning to go and asked about places, especially the Greek ruins in Agrigento and Selinunte in the southern part of the island. "It's hard to imagine so many temples and temple ruins in such a condensed area," Brian said as he took a sip from his glass of red wine. "Go now. Before it becomes a Disney venue."

We went out four times over a period of three months. After the first time, he picked me up at my house and each time, after dinner, we'd come back and talk in my living room, sitting next to each other on the sofa. On our second or third date, he told me he'd just spent a week with his daughter, her husband, and the grandchildren in Brooklyn. "I don't see them as much as I'd like, but since my wife died, we've spent more time together. They keep tabs on me." I wanted to share in the keeping of tabs.

The topic—family, friends, theater, books, travel, an unexpected anecdote, whatever—didn't matter. I was aware that we were beginning to make a connection. But no matter how pleasant an evening had been, Brian was guarded about discussing his life and never said when he'd be returning to California or suggested I visit him back East. I wondered if he might be living with a woman in New York, but he didn't come across as a Lothario. Still, after each of our dates, he kept me guessing when he'd be back. I wondered where I stood with him or, worse yet, whether I had any standing at all.

We were in the foyer of my living room by the front door when he kissed me good-bye after our fourth date (I'd counted; it was kiss number three, since he'd been a proper non-kissing gentleman on our first date). His kiss was warm, slow, and intimate. My response was equally warm and slow. I asked him when he would be coming back, knowing he would say he didn't know, and that is exactly what he said. I was pissed. I wanted to take him by the arm, look him in the face, and ask, "How can we talk and laugh so easily for three and a half hours and kiss the way we just did and not talk about your next visit?" But, confused, curious, nervous, angry, hurt, and vulnerable, I froze up and pulled away. I said good-bye tersely and didn't walk him to his car, as I had always done before. I closed the door and turned off the porch light before Brian pulled away from the curb. He didn't call me again.

The second man was local. Stan was endearing and teeming with boyish energy and enthusiasm. He was the most physically attractive man I had met. Unfortunately, although legally separated, he was still emotionally connected to his estranged alcoholic wife. He mentioned to me one time too many that she was strikingly beautiful. One night he let it slip out that he had "gone to pick up our son, stayed for dinner, and spent the night." He stuttered briefly as he caught himself and changed the subject, saying, "My son is having a hard time with our separation. He wants to come live with me, and I would be happy to have him."

Stan was game for us to keep dating, but I sensed I would be his training wheels. I had no desire to witness the dissolution of his marriage and the effects on his college-age son. It would be long and painful. I was still hurting and feeling confused about the missed connection with Brian. I listened to my dented heart and stopped seeing Stan.

Dashed expectations. Blighted hopes. I pulled the plug on the e-sites.

After all, my search for a partner wasn't the entire focus of my life. For years I had been expanding my range of volunteer work with animal rescue shelters in Berkeley. I'd maintained and grown my circle of friends and capitalized on my interests in Spanish and travel. I was working with two medical organizations as a medical interpreter: Rotaplast, a Rotary-sponsored organization based in San Francisco that runs surgical missions in Latin America, operating on children to correct cleft palates and cleft lips, and ASAPROSAR, a health clinic in El Salvador that works with UC Berkeley's School of Public Health on dental hygiene and nutrition missions for children in villages outside of Santa Ana. I'd picked up medical terminology so I could write manuals, charts, and posters in Spanish for the English-speaking doctors and nurses. My trips to Peru, Venezuela, El Salvador, and Nicaragua brought new friends into my life.

I kept up with girlfriends and former work colleagues in the Bay Area. I never missed my monthly women's reading group, for which our list of books read and discussed was fast approaching three hundred. I signed up for brain-nurturing classes at the Osher Lifelong Learning Center at UC Berkeley and took courses on Scandinavian fiction, dream analysis, documentary filmmaking, and the history of rock and roll.

Finally, I joined Berkeley Rotary, at the recommendation of a former work colleague who knew the club was seeking an interpreter to help with school-building projects in the state of Nayarit, north of Puerto Vallarta. I made two construction trips, interpreting at hardware and paint stores, teaching English to high schoolers, and scraping walls and painting classrooms in ninety-degree weather. The teaching was my favorite part (along with the nightly margaritas on the beach, with mariachi musicians playing in the open-air restaurants). I had taken a trove of stickers with me and, as students responded to my questions in English, correctly or not, I decorated their cheeks and foreheads. They vied to get the most stickers—suns, moons, princesses, boats, flowers, birds—the design didn't matter, even to the macho boys. One girl with a radiant smile sought me out the last day of class and confided she wanted me to be her regular English teacher. "I'm going to keep my stickers on till they fall off," she told me shyly.

Following the devastation of Hurricane Katrina on August 29, 2005, members of Berkeley Rotary postponed their 2006

Mexico trip, opting instead to rehabilitate a Katrina-damaged school. I connected the Berkeley Rotarians with a former neighbor of mine, a New Orleans Rotarian who'd returned to the waterlogged city. He knew which other Rotarians had trickled back and where they had found housing. Ultimately, Rotarians from my two hometowns worked together over two summers to restore Warren Easton High School, the oldest public school in the city.

Before we left for our first trip to New Orleans, a Berkeley Rotarian took me aside. "We're a bit nervous. Are the Rotarians down there good ol' boys? We're worried we won't have much in common." I assured him we'd all be fine.

And we were. Once the Berkeley Left Coasters met the New Orleans Rotarians, the Berkeleyites fell in love with their open-minded, warmhearted, service-oriented Southern counterparts. We sweated side by side in the middle of the torturously muggy summer, throwing out rotting desks and chairs; tearing out mold-blackened walls and bulletin boards; replacing electrical wiring, sockets, and lights; tiling floors; and installing new computers. We hammered, sanded, painted, and caulked, with our only luxuries being boxes of warm bottled water, a generator with one cord leading into the building, and a Porta-Potty.

"You guys are astonishing!" the New Orleanians exclaimed as they worked alongside sweat-soaked Californians two summers in a row without air conditioning or fans. "We expected hippies with beards and Birkenstocks, maybe even some marijuana," one man confided. By the time the high school was back in business, the non-good ol' boys and non-hippies were soul brothers and sisters, emailing and phoning to stay in touch, a practice they maintain to this day.

By 2016, with friends old and new, life had become rich in many ways, even if I wasn't always grateful for this abundance.

It had been fourteen years and counting since Matt had died. I still bounced out of bed in the morning without an ache or pain. Friends and meaningful activities fed my mind and fueled my body and soul. But I continued peering over at the empty side of the bed, a space I longed to fill. I missed having a soul mate.

4

"DON'T GIVE UP"

(Peter Gabriel version)

I faced three choices: dump my search entirely, ramp it down, or change the way I was searching.

Quitting for good wasn't acceptable, given my hard wiring. Call me hard-headed (Steve: "And stubborn and impractical." Sweet Pea: "Yet delightfully optimistic.") or unreasonable (Steve: "And half-baked and illogical." Sweet Pea: "Hey. Her head is screwed on straight."). But I've finally learned that disappointments are often temporary. Hadn't I seen how narrow a thread could turn into a lifeline? If the postage rates hadn't increased by two cents back in 1978, and if Matt hadn't sent me his only photo of him and his dog, and if I hadn't loved dogs enough to return the photo to a man I had relegated to the MAYBE pile, my life would have taken a different turn. Why couldn't there be another slender thread? So after each disappointment, I let myself have a brief respite to bounce back, and then I kept going.

Maybe if I invested less emotional energy, I wouldn't feel as discouraged. (Steve: "A ramped-down approach is quitting halfway." Sweet Pea: "But she keeps going. Remember when she learned to ski?") I'm from the give-it-your-all school. When I learned to ski in my early twenties, I fell countless times as my long skis crossed and recrossed. Over and over, I removed my skis, scrambled back up, and reattached them to my boots, by myself since my friends had headed for the advanced slopes. One particular day I fell off the T-bar twice, to the scornful looks of even the bunny-slope beginners. Later that afternoon, I caught my skis in the tow rope, forcing the attendant to stop the entire operation. I waited twenty minutes to get back in line, hoping those who had witnessed my embarrassing mishap had moved on. This time I succeeded. I got back on and let go of the tow rope without falling. By the end of the week, I had become a low-level intermediate skier, able to navigate the T-bar, tow rope, and chairlift without tumbles and falls.

This same determination helped me raise my daughter post-divorce, initially without child support, and ultimately enabled me to risk leaving a job with benefits but minimal future potential and accept a short-term hourly position with career possibilities. My DNA pointed me toward the third choice, changing my approach, though I didn't know how to go about it.

I thought about my former professional turn as a recruiter. In 1981, after four years as a vocational rehabilitation counselor, I was offered a job as midnight shift interviewer at the Federal Reserve Bank of San Francisco. It was a six-month contract, with no assurance of continued work. I was frightened to quit a job with health benefits and gamble on an iffy chance for career advancement, but even more frightened not to. Matt made it easy. Without a second's thought, he put his arms on my shoulders and said, using his pet name for me, "Sarah, you go in there and beat Notre Dame." I didn't know what beating Notre Dame had to do with accepting the job (maybe if he'd said "win one for the Gipper"), but I knew he was telling me to go for it.

I took the temporary job, and, when the six months ended, I was hired as a regular employee and eventually became regional vice president of human resources and public affairs. I had to learn the language of economists, bank regulators, financial analysts, and banking operations officers. Regardless of the positions I held, however, in my core I was always a recruiter, working to find the right person for the right spot for the organization.

At the Federal Reserve, when a department had an opening, I gathered as much information from the hiring manager as I could to scope out the department's staffing needs. I asked questions about the skill set the successful applicant should have. I decided to apply my recruiting experience to dating.

And so, on a spring morning in March 2016, I sat at my desk with a cup of coffee and a blank sheet of paper while my two rescue mutts competed for my attention. As I patted their heads and scratched them behind the ears, I completed step one of my personalized recruiting process, the job description. I listed the attributes I wanted in a life partner.

- Emotionally stable, Economically stable
- Spiritual
- Religious (not or not very)
- Adventurous, Active, Animal friendly, Aging gently
- Physically fit, Politically liberal
- Monkey business
- Travel aficionado
- Intelligent, Intellectual

An addicted daily Jumble practitioner of long standing, I was instantaneously aware of four almost-perfect anagrams popping out from the first letter of each attribute:

AIMSTAR (no E or P)
MATEPAIR (no S)
MASERATI (no P), and
PASTRAMI (no E)

AIMSTAR was good. It conveyed a sense of focus and direction, as well as astral luminosity, but it sounded like the name of a cell phone company in Central America. MATEPAIR seemed pedestrian, although relevant to a personals search. I'm not big on cars and most especially not fancy cars, so MASERATI was out. PASTRAMI tickled my funny bone. I broke out into a smile and kept smiling. PASTRAMI was juicy, appealing, and lighthearted, even to a quasi-vegetarian. And, best of all, it was silly.

But this description would only be useful if I could target a way to reach guys with PASTRAMI attributes. My first thought was to ask people to help me find them, but who? My family and close friends had heard more than enough about how much I missed Matt. They already knew all about my Internet-based personals search. I felt sure I'd exhausted their good will and their resources. Besides, when I'd asked my family and close friends if they knew any available men, they'd routinely say, "Yes, but there's a reason they're available." Or "No, but I know lots of women who are looking." Most depressing were the frequent responses from people who'd known Matt well: "Sallie, I can't imagine you with anyone but Matt. He was larger than life." I knew that. And it pissed me off to hear them say it. And broke my heart.

While I felt guilty about not revealing my PASTRAMI search to those closest and dearest to me, I needed to go to people I hadn't previously approached, many of whom probably weren't even aware I was seeking a life partner. I would enlist people who knew me well enough to know what kind of person I would be attracted to and who might be attracted to me. A number of Berkeley Rotary Club members fit this category—we'd parked cars at the annual Berkeley Kite Festival, delivered dictionaries to all third graders in the city's public school system, set up and taken down tables and chairs at conferences, and danced at holiday parties. I'd include a few people in a network of doctors and nurses associated with the cervical cancer prevention organization with which I'd begun volunteering in Nicaragua and El Salvador. They knew me well. We'd taped together black garbage bags and hung them on ropes to provide privacy curtains in makeshift clinics. We'd spent hours in a cramped van in the middle of a jungle, singing folk songs and swapping stories about our day. We'd shared many a late-night bottle of local beer. Finally, I would approach some of the wait staff at my favorite restaurants. Not inclined to eat dinner by myself night after night, I would often go to one of my favorite walking-distance restaurants, sit at the bar, read my Kindle, and chat with the employees, most often the bartenders. We'd talk about books, music, our dogs (Berkeley abounds with animal lovers), and politics. Maybe my age-harmonious male counterpart was doing the same with my friendly bartenders on nights I wasn't there, and one of them would introduce us.

To encourage participation, I would offer a finder's fee. For over a decade, I have been teaching conversational Spanish every week to a dentist who had worked pro bono with me in El Salvador and who likes to be able to talk to her patients in their language. I charge her my hourly tutoring fee, but she pays it to a nonprofit of my choice. I decided to use this approach for my soul mate search; if a mutually committed and fulfilling relationship with a "PASTRAMI Candidate" lasted for a year, I would pay five thousand dollars to a charitable organization chosen by the person who referred the successful Candidate.

How to get the word out to these potential "PASTRAMI Love Liaisons" was presumably the easy part. Instead of using the web to post my profile on established dating sites and contact men who'd done the same, I would set up a personalized website and spread the word, one friend at a time. I was brewing a plan. My sister, formerly an editor of *Mademoiselle* and editor-in-chief of *Louisiana Magazine*, writes and edits masterfully. She has her own business website, and her son Clayton is her web designer and webmaster. I knew they would not only help me think out the steps to design my site, they'd put the website together. My three-person Team PASTRAMI would consist of a creative consultant (Virginia), editor and content manager (Virginia), and designer and technical troubleshooter (Clayton), overseen by Team PASTRAMI's CEO/seeker-in-chief and writer (me). All I had to do was enlist them in my scheme.

The idea gestated in my mind for several months. Sweet Pea and Steve had a field day.

Steve: "It's stupid. She'll fail with PASTRAMI. And make a fool of herself."

Sweet Pea: "She has the chutzpah to carry it off. Anyway, you can't stop her. She's always gone for what she wanted."

Steve: "Yes, but she was younger then. Now she's too old."

Sweet Pea: "Her heart is young. She can still rock and roll."

Steve: "If it were in the cards for her to meet someone, she'd have met him by now. Anyway, what does she need a man for?"

Sweet Pea: "It isn't about need. It's about want. She wants to love again."

I listened to Sweet Pea and ignored Steve. I tried to figure out how to make PASTRAMI work and why I wanted it to work. It seemed pretty simple. I wanted to be happy, as happy as I had been with Matt. As he was dying, he had said, "Sarah, I want you to have a rich life when I'm gone." After his death, happiness seemed a distant land I would never revisit, but now PASTRAMI offered hope: the shiny penny vehicle leading back to the possibility of time, place, and opportunity coming together. But, for the time being, I kept my idea to myself.

In late May 2016, I broke my silence. I spilled the beans about PASTRAMI to my sister, Virginia. I needed input, especially from someone who knew me well and who, if she endorsed the concept, would become my dedicated PASTRAMI colleague. My sister was a safe choice—she lives far away and wouldn't be around to watch me wrestle with my attacks of indecision. She is more of a "go for it" person than I am, and she knows me to be gutsy at times and diffident at others.

As the president and cofounder of a global nonprofit organization that facilitates economic opportunities for women entrepreneurs, Virginia travels throughout Asia, Europe, Latin America, Africa, and the Middle East, developing client–supplier relationships, promoting policies, and speaking at international conferences. She was returning to Washington, DC, from a business trip to China and had a four-hour layover at San Francisco Airport. We met at the International Terminal for a sisterly catch-up. Toward the end of our visit, with less than an hour before she'd have to go back through the security area, she asked for a status report on my online dating. "I've given up on it, Gin," I said, using her nickname from when we were kids. "It hasn't gone anywhere since I broke off with Keith. I'm not finding anyone who meets me even halfway. I would rather be alone than with someone who leaves me hungry." I told her about my letdowns, lackluster dates, the various not-even-close non-adventures. She laughed at some of my encounters and commiserated about others.

We were short on time, and I wanted to use the remaining minutes well. "But I have an idea to bounce off you. I have mixed feelings about this and want your honest reaction. And, if I decide to do it, I need you and Clayton in on it. I can't do it without you." As travelers passed us, heading out of the terminal to catch taxis and shuttles, and others, fresher and less rumpled, walked toward the security area to catch flights to foreign countries, I spoke about the PASTRAMI letters, the Candidates whose lights I hoped to find hidden under bushels, the personalized PASTRAMI website, the donation to a nonprofit, and my qualms about being able to carry it off.

The more I explained my idea, the more my sister lit up. In the midst of the scores of travelers maneuvering their suitcases and chattering on their cell phones, we were in high school again—she sixteen to my fourteen, talking about boys and plotting how to get them to notice us. "Oh, Sallie," she said with her eyes filled with amusement and approval, "it's a trip and a half." The prospect of my waging an all-out recruitment effort to find guys—or one guy—who embodied the PASTRAMI attributes set her off into a full-body, full-belly laugh. She put both hands over her mouth, to keep from spewing out her coffee as she howled, "PASTRAMI! PASTRAMI! Sallie, it's fabulous. It's outrageous and totally ridiculous. PASTRAMI! You can absolutely do this."

5

"WITH A LITTLE HELP FROM MY FRIENDS"

(The Beatles version)

My sister's over-the-top reaction at the airport was just what I needed. What I hadn't expected was her assuming the role of impassioned cheerleader. She referred to it as "charismatizing" me, providing enthusiastic moral support. In our early years, Virginia had very much been the older sister, taking her innocent younger sibling by the hand and guiding her down life's pathway. She taught me the facts of life when my parents remained silent on the subject. She showed me how to shave my legs with a double-edged safety razor, the kind that screwed into my dad's blade holder, without cutting myself. She helped me buy my first bra and prepared me for dealing with the embarrassing need for Kotex and ultimately Tampax. We explored the various techniques of making out with boys and debated what a nice girl would and wouldn't let her boyfriend do (I was more prudish than she was). Even without firsthand experience, she extolled the attractions of French kissing, a practice I, as a teenager, found disgusting. Why would any girl let a guy put his tongue in her mouth? She also explained to me what a hickey was—a "monkey bite," she called it—and again I was dumbfounded (and still am) as to why being bitten and bruised was considered sexy. I had counted on her sisterly wisdom back then and now was counting on it again for upping my chances for romantic encounters at seventy-plus.

I began approaching a few other people to get their reactions to my idea for a website—though I was apprehensive they might think I'd taken leave of my senses. When I was in the Los Angeles area, I talked to Tracy, a lawyer and single mom. Her widowed father and I had begun dating a year after my divorce from Daniel. At the time Tracy was in fourth grade, and her brother, Andrew, was in first grade. Their mother had died of Hodgkin's lymphoma several years before.

A coworker of mine introduced us; Bob was her husband's boss at a big San Francisco law firm. Both she and her husband found him charming, intelligent, kind, and a "devoted father and all-around good person, somewhat of a Renaissance man. And his kids are darling." That was certainly how it seemed when we met and while we were dating. Heather and I began spending weekends with them. The three children got along, and Heather considered them her brother and sister. We felt like a family, and life was good.

Now it's *True Confessions* time. I'm revealing a secret I've kept for too long from even my closest friends. I ended up marrying Bob.

He proposed after about a year of dating. I accepted, and we set a date. A month before our marriage, Heather and I moved in with him, Tracy, and Andrew. I quickly came to realize that the glasses of wine we'd each enjoyed drinking in front of the fire on weekends were a full bottle or more—his, not mine—every night after we came home from work. He drank even more on the weekends, which he had not done before, at least not in front of me.

Increasingly uncomfortable about going forward with the wedding, I suggested we postpone it. Bob became furious and said, if I chose to move the date, we wouldn't see each other again. I can't believe I caved in, but I did. I adored Tracy and Andrew, Heather loved them as well, and I cared for Bob deeply. I couldn't imagine having the children lose another mother.

I wondered if I was overreacting. I called my parents to help me figure out how to handle this. Mom, who'd suffered for years living with a drinking, womanizing father, surprised me by commenting I was taking the drinking too seriously. "Sal, he loves you and Heather, and you seemed so happy together when we visited you. You're being too dramatic. It'll be fine." The following week I called again and got the same message. I shut down.

We got married in his home in Berkeley. Bob's mother stayed with the kids while we went to the elegant Stanford Court on Nob Hill for a two-day San Francisco honeymoon weekend. The first evening Bob drank a bottle and a half of champagne. After he fell asleep, I poured the rest of the second bottle down the sink. I have no memory of the second day and night. I spent the next month wondering how I could ever leave Tracy and Andrew. But I had to, and it would only be harder the longer I waited. I found an apartment for Heather and me. Bob said that I would no longer be welcome to see his children.

I saw a psychologist to see if I qualified for an annulment based on being "emotionally fragile." The answer was no—I was sane. Sane but horrified that I had allowed myself to be blackmailed. I filed for divorce. The marriage had lasted five weeks.

When we met at the one-year point to finalize the divorce, Bob told me he knew he had been pressuring me. Not only had he thought it would work, he thought it was an appropriate strategy. He also said he'd never "lost a client before" in his practice. I remember being astonished and saying, "Bob, I wasn't a client. I was your wife!" He didn't seem to understand they weren't the same thing. I'm still humiliated by the whole experience.

When Tracy was in her late twenties, she contacted me. She and her father had fallen out over his continued drinking and his increasingly dictatorial behavior toward her. Within an hour, most of which we spent crying and hugging, we had reestablished our mother–daughter bond. Some years ago, her young son Zach was with us at breakfast as we talked and laughed. After watching us quietly for ten minutes, he asked, "Mommy, is she your mommy?"

"No, but she should have been," Tracy answered, hugging him.

"Zach, I wish I had been. I wanted to be," I said, with tears trickling down my face.

So it meant a lot to me when Tracy said, "Yes, it's crazy and yes, you can do it." She added, "But you don't want any stuffed shirts—no one in black and white. You do things in color. Find someone who makes you laugh." She suggested I post my quest on social media and advised me to hire a graduate marketing student to target the Candidate pool and review responses. "You're going to be swamped," she said.

More friends lit up when I introduced the concept—especially when I handed them the list of PASTRAMI attributes. They followed up with specific input. "Avoid the leeches out there, don't waste your time. There are too many jerks, married men on the prowl, and criminals trying to make money off lonely women. I don't want you to become a victim," Tina, a close Rotarian friend said, advising against social media. She had no idea how much her comments hit a raw nerve.

One of my pre-PASTRAMI online encounters had been Josh, a PhD geophysicist living in San Francisco, the CEO of a Texas-based oil and gas exploration company. He was semiretired and grooming his son, also a geophysicist, to take over the business. I was about to leave town, and Josh and I couldn't squeeze in a coffee meeting before my departure, although we spoke on the phone a few times. After I left California, he emailed that he had to go to Dubai for a week; he expected to be back before I returned: "I've enjoyed our phone chats and can't wait to meet you in person. It will be good."

In the first email he sent me from Dubai, Josh included photos of himself playing soccer, a lively senior enjoying himself with his friends; a picture of the work site with drilling platforms, trucks, and unidentified equipment of various sizes and shapes; and a cedar door he'd carved the previous summer, depicting a pomegranate tree. He planned to put the door on the front entrance of his house in San Francisco upon his return. This Renaissance man ended the email saying, "I haven't traveled much recently, but hope, in time, to share time traveling with a partner."

Over the next week, he continued to email photos of himself at the work site and views of Dubai taken from his hotel window. He wrote about the technicalities of conducting seismic surveys for oil and gas exploration and of zones with hydrocarbon potential—and, refreshingly, asked questions about my trip. Josh showed concern when I'd mentioned I'd come down with a nasty cold.

In his next email, he wrote that there'd been an explosion. Seven field workers—he called them roustabouts—were injured, and the authorities had levied fines on his company. The news kept getting worse. Two workers had died. The fines had escalated, and the authorities accused his company of having inadequate safety procedures, so Josh would be responsible for death compensation payments. His passport had been confiscated. Next he wrote, "Things are at a standstill since the accident. I stay in my hotel and don't go out. I have paid eighty percent of the fine." For the first time he called me "babe" and "honey," which struck me as out of character with his previous emails and calls. I became suspicious of the drama—it felt false, invented. Josh asked that I phone him right away. I didn't.

An hour later I had an email from him, asking for twenty-five thousand dollars to retrieve his passport and pay the rest of the fines and reclaim his equipment. He emailed me his Bank of America routing and account numbers and assured me he couldn't wait to meet when we both returned to the Bay Area. When he didn't hear from me, he emailed again, asking when the money would arrive. I Googled his website, only to find his oil and gas exploration company no longer appeared on the Internet.

I felt hurt, angry, disappointed, and spectacularly foolish. I hadn't seen the request for money coming till he asked me to phone him. I'd become the pathetic cliché I'd read about: the older, lonely woman, widowed or divorced, preyed upon by a man who works his way into her confidence and her bank account.

And he wasn't the only one. Monroe, a divorced architect in San Jose, was new to the world of e-dating; his observations about his search paralleled mine. "I guess it's about kissing a lot of frogs before meeting the right person," he wrote. "I understand that loving is not about how much we have in the beginning, but how much we can build into it as time goes by. I want more than just a woman in my life, I want a best friend." There was no denying his eloquence. "Some say love is like a butterfly in the belly," he said in another email. "I say it's the feeling you get from being with someone and you like her so much you want to spend the rest of your life living with her. I know what I want—an equal partner—and won't waste your time. I give a hundred and ten percent." His words reinvigorated my ebbing supply of optimism. Coffee with this man seemed promising but would have to wait a few weeks.

Monroe had been selected over the other five bidders for a mall project in Glasgow, but was dismayed to learn that, as a foreigner, he needed to purchase a special permit to begin work in Scotland. He needed an additional ten thousand dollars, or local officials would select the runner-up bid. He hated to ask me for a one-week loan but assured me of repayment: "You have nothing to be worried about."

This was all too familiar—a stranger's unanticipated debt involving a major project in a foreign country complete with a promise to make good. "I wish I knew you," I responded skeptically. "I wish I had seen your face, your eyes. Because then I'd know if I could believe you. But, sight unseen, I don't. This is a scam." I ended, "If I'm wrong, please contact me when you're back in California." I wasn't surprised there was no response. **(Steve: "She should have seen it coming." Sweet Pea: "At least she didn't send the money.")**

Finally I shared PASTRAMI with my stepdaughter Beth, and her husband, Steve. The three of us explore local restaurants every few months. We also share an affinity for cats. Beth has a PhD in American history from Berkeley, is a published author, and works as a public relations executive in San Francisco. Endlessly creative, Beth invariably has multiple house and garden projects underway. Steve is an artist, a financial investment guru, a wine broker, an accomplished chef, and, since Matt's death, *paterfamilias* of the clan.

"It's brave, it's creative and it's 'out there,'" Beth said as she, Steve, and I sipped wine at an Oakland restaurant. She added a second suggestion. "Sarah," she said, addressing me with the nickname her father used, "don't limit yourself to the Bay Area and New Orleans. You'll be excluding worthy possibilities." Finally, as they gazed at the PASTRAMI list, she and Steve looked at each other and grinned. "Animal friendly?" Steve laughed. "That's NOT strong enough to match up with you. You need to change it to 'Animal lover.'"

"Or, to be honest, 'crazy cat and dog person,'" Beth quipped.

Steve piped up, "Maybe 'fanatic.'" So I changed the wording to "lover," knowing full well that both their descriptions were spot-on.

While I was getting input from friends, I was writing text and sending images to Virginia and Clayton. We expanded the number of PASTRAMI attributes, bringing back Emotionally and Economically stable and adding Tender (yet strong), and Communicative/Culturally oriented. Now it was PASTRAMI ETC.

By August 2016, the PASTRAMI site was poised for its rollout. But first, I wanted critiques from Tina and Shawn, my Rotarian PASTRAMI confidants. Tina wrote her feedback: "Too many pictures of pastrami sandwiches. You take too long getting to the point. Make it clear right away this is a search for a life partner. Too many statistics." I was amused at this, coming from a biochemist. We sat at my dining room table, drinking tea as she summarized her well-organized comments: "Delete the age bracket for the Candidates—what if you miss out on someone because he's one year too young or too old and doesn't put himself in the running? That's the way an engineer thinks. Don't screen out the engineers."

Pal Shawn was equally candid. Twenty years younger than

I, Shawn always has a mischievous gleam in his eyes. From the time we met several years ago, we've nurtured our shared sense of humor and have sought each other out at Rotary Club and board meetings, where we have occasionally been encouraged to laugh less and pay more attention to agenda topics. "It's confusing," he began. "Sometimes you say 'I' and sometimes you say 'Sallie' or 'she.' Pick one or the other," he advised. He was skeptical of my offering a finder's fee to a nonprofit. "Let the money simmer for now," he advised. "Don't mix the search-for-love effort with a financial incentive. And be realistic, be flexible—you're looking for your dream partner, but you're not going to find a hundred percent." He nixed photos he found too serious. "You're more enthusiastic and energetic than that. Ditch these," he instructed, pointing to two schoolmarmish images. Looking at the "elevator pitch" card nephew Clayton had designed, Shawn advised, "Here you're saying, 'Help me find someone.' Your message should be less 'Help me out' and more 'Be someone your friend thanks for introducing him to Sallie.'"

Shawn's comment got me out of my head and into the perspective of the people whose help I was seeking—how could I frame the appeal to motivate them to matchmake? To make it a win-win all around, not just for me? I changed the wording to, "Be a PASTRAMI Love Liaison—help your friend, friend of a friend, relative, or colleague look forward to his Saturday nights . . . and all days and nights . . . again."

To beef up the "About the Ideal PASTRAMI Candidate" section, Clayton and I surfed the Internet for photos of what I envisioned my Eureka Man would look like: a composite of age-appropriate men featured in *GQ* (dressed casually, not in a tux), *Field and Stream* (fit and outdoorsy, without the guns), and *Travel and Leisure* (ideally, in REI hiking garb with a canine at his side). Clayton and I Googled for hours, seeking images of the hundred percent PASTRAMI guy.

Unbeknownst to me, Clayton decided my spirits needed raising and began looking for what he called "the Failed Candidate." He found images of men he knew would make me laugh. The most memorable was a balding naked man in his mid-forties with an extra-hairy chest and belly, sitting in a bathtub filled to the brim with soapy water such that, mercifully, no private body parts were visible. He was obese, with his stomach protruding above the water line and his belly button showing. He held a gun in one hand and a rubber ducky in the other.

One chilly Berkeley morning, before leaving the house for my daily coffee and dog-walking ritual, I turned on my computer and opened an email from Clayton who had found some photos for me to consider, this time in all seriousness: two of them were taken on a beach with a lake or ocean in the background and the mystery man's back to the camera. One was shot at dawn with a rocky cliff on the left; the other was taken at sunset, with trees in the near distance and mountains in the background. The third was an image of a man kneeling down, the side of his face in shadows, with the sun setting in the background. He was stretching his arms and hands out to his dog, a majestic German shepherd that reminded me of my shepherd-headed, Dachshund-bodied Clementine. That was Eureka Man.

To the dismay of my impatient dogs, I delayed leaving the house and phoned my nephew. "Clayton, you've nailed it," I announced. "You found him. Now find him for real—or his father or his favorite uncle—and I won't have to look any further," I said, wishing it could be that easy.

In late October 2016, PASTRAMI went live. Along with printing the elevator pitch cards, I drew up a list of sixty-five possible Love Liaisons. On the list were a number of Berkeley Rotarians, former work colleagues, my hair stylist (a friend of thirty years), dental hygienist, realtor (a friend of almost forty years), and financial planner (a friend of ten years). I included a congenial breakfast companion at my morning coffee shop and various restaurant managers and waitstaff I knew well. All were people who had a sense of who I am, what I think, and how I live. They were likely to know the type of men I wanted to meet. Equally important, they hadn't known Matt well. Most of them had never met him. The sole exceptions were my four stepdaughters. I included them on the off chance that their friends' fathers might be available. They knew how deeply I had loved their father and had often told me they hoped I would find another life companion.

Now came the part I dreaded—asking people to go on the prowl on my behalf. I hate asking for help, especially asking for money, even for charitable organizations. In the past, I've been so miserable when I had to raise money for the Oakland SPCA and my volunteer medical nonprofit organizations that I would donate the amounts myself. PASTRAMI seemed even harder. I'd be begging for myself, not for a cause that would make the world a better place.

"I'm embarking on a quest," I began haltingly, "seeking a life partner." As I practiced my speech at home, in the uncritical presence of the dogs, I groaned. "Embarking on" sounded like something a ship's captain would say over a loudspeaker, as passengers schlepped their roller bags up the gangplank on a cruise ship. "Life partner" didn't sound right either, but it was better than saying "I'm looking for a soul mate," which, even if it sounded too spiritual, was exactly what I wanted. I wordsmithed my pitch for a couple of days until the lightning of self-realization struck: *Shazam*! It didn't matter what I said as long as I felt saucy and self-assured when I said it.

I kept practicing, going more for the feeling than the words. I knew it would all depend on how confident I was feeling and to what extent a friend's eyes would light up when I began my spiel. I imagined saying, "Hi. I want to talk with you about something I'm doing. It's a personalized online personals search I'm starting to find a life partner. I call it PASTRAMI, shorthand for what I'm looking for in a man: P for physically active, the A's for adventurous. The M's my favorite—someone with a good sense of monkey business. I'd like your help. The card inside this envelope tells you about it, and there's more on my website—the link's on the card."

Fortified with a packet of PASTRAMI pitch cards in my purse and in the glove compartment of my car, I went to meetings and appointments, intending to engage one or two individuals on my list. My plan was to take him or her or them aside for a private chat or make a date to meet later, but that wasn't always possible. Often the potential Love Liaison was talking in a group or engrossed in a committee meeting and couldn't be enticed to a secluded nook. But even when conditions were auspicious, I might lose my nerve. Asking friends to matchmake turned out to be twice as tough as I'd imagined. Sometimes it was just easier to email a prospective Love Liaison instead.

With time, it got easier to make my pitch, but it was never easy. When I approached friends, my smile rarely came off as one hundred percent sincere. If my listeners smiled back—and they usually did—I relaxed. More and more, after hearing the PASTRAMI rap, my listeners were full-out grinning as I ended, "The website—it's on the card inside—is where you'll get the total PASTRAMI," and added, "And, to sweeten the deal, there's a five-thousand-dollar donation to a nonprofit of your choice if this works. I hope you'll participate." I'd hand over the personally addressed hot pink envelope, with a card inside chock-full of exclamation points, "Be a PASTRAMI Love Liaison! Refer a PASTRAMI Candidate! I'm itching to write that check!"

I was astonished by the out-of-the-ballpark responses. My hair stylist, Becca, one of the first to receive a card, opened it at the salon and broke into a grin. "Sallie, this is so cool. I know you think I'm woo-woo. But I really believe you can change the atoms by what you send out, and you can then determine what atoms come back to you." She was swinging her arms like a little girl. "This is going to happen to you in 2017."

Two weeks later, I gave the manager at my morning coffee shop a PASTRAMI card. "It's fun to think about PASTRAMI," she told me the next morning. "I looked at your site and keep thinking about it. And, instead of thinking of someone looking for love, I think about a pastrami sandwich. Yum. I walk around thinking 'pastrami' and keeping my eyes open."

The most amusing response came from a married friend, who is an innocent, if avid, flirt. Two days after I invited him to be a Love Liaison, Jake emailed a two-page response: "I DID look at all the criteria. However, there are SOOOO many. In light of this, I redefined them to tilt the score ever so slightly in my favor. P = persistent. I have been after you for years. A = available. But the way you so precisely define it, I am a little short here. Is there such a thing as partial credit? S = substitute. I'm willing to fill in as you wait for Mr. Right to materialize." He proceeded through the rest of the PASTRAMI ETC letters in a similar vein, getting to the second T. "T = tickled. I am tickled you asked me to help you find Mr. Right. I actually know the perfect man for you and will check to see if he's available. Lives in Los Angeles and his wife died three years ago. He's a terrific guy with a great sense of humor." He ended with "C = checking. I am checking to see if he is dating anyone or not."

My heart surged at the idea of a pre-screened Mr. Right materializing so quickly through the efforts of someone I admired and valued. Manna from PASTRAMI heaven was about to fall into my lap. I was tempted to stop handing out any more hot pink envelopes till I heard more about Los Angeles Mr. Right, but didn't want to lose momentum. Whether this man and I worked out or not, I was on the right track—finding people to take on the matchmaker role, vet the Candidates, and filter out those I had wasted so much time meeting in the past. I told myself not to hope, but I couldn't help it.

Harsh reality intruded. Jake emailed me a week later, "Well, so much for the perfect guy. While his wife was dying, he fell trying to catch her and injured his back. Since then, he's been in constant pain, taking medication that's affecting his memory. He's got a part-time caretaker and can't drive to the corner store, much less start up a relationship."

Damnation, I thought to myself, although, to be honest, my monosyllabic expletive was less sanitized.

In spite of the glowing reactions to PASTRAMI, by year-end 2016 I'd contacted only half of the sixty-five prospective Love Liaisons on my list. PASTRAMI went into hibernation through the 2016 holidays and into the first part of the new year. During that time, I found I was still brooding about Brian. I had been smitten, wanted more, and was hurt by his disappearance. He hadn't broken my heart, but he had stomped on it. Had I misinterpreted his feelings for me, taking them for romantic when they were merely friendly? Perplexed about why we had reached a dead end, I emailed him.

It was easy to tell him about my feelings for him, the passage of time stripping away my self-protectiveness. "I enjoyed knowing you and admit to being disappointed that, for reasons only you know, we didn't click," I wrote. "I assume the chemistry wasn't there for you. It was for me. At this point, I have nothing to lose by telling you that I liked you a lot. With time, I would have come to love you." I continued, surprising myself with the unrestrained admission, "I thought we had possibilities that never developed. You didn't seem open to getting to know me better. For reasons I don't understand, you shut me out and never got to know the real me." I told him I'd stopped doing the online personals, told him about PASTRAMI, and gave him the link. I ended by saying, "If you have any curiosity or are intrigued by who I am, it's on my website. Regardless of what happens, I hope you are well."

He replied fairly quickly. "Sallie, it was really geography and travel schedules, not that I wasn't enjoying our time together or because of a lack of click," he responded. "Honestly, I wasn't sure how much click there was on your side, and that might have caused some reluctance on my part to take a risk. We clearly have the same love of life and interest in adventure, travel, and the arts. Had we lived physically closer, I'm sure things would have happened. Looking back, I think I dropped the ball and was a bit rude in doing so. And I'm sorry about that. You are terrific, and I apologize. Later last year, I met someone close by, and we have started doing more and more together. I would be glad to count you as a long-term California friend and raise an occasional glass of wine together. Certainly, I wish you the best in everything."

In my second email, I responded to his questioning whether there was click on my end, "I thought it was obvious. On each trip you made, I asked whether we could get together again before you left and also when you would be coming back. You invariably said 'no' and 'I don't know.' I thought I kissed you back somewhat shamelessly. It's futile to say it now, but I was much more flexible geographically than you imagined." I demurred on his offer to share a glass of wine but thanked him for his candid and flattering response and wished him the best as well.

I was relieved I'd had the nerve to ask why a relationship hadn't developed, but his response sent me into a tailspin of overthinking. Yes, I could have said as he left my house at the end of one of our evenings together, "I like you, but have no idea how you feel about me. It hurts to say good-bye and not know when I'll see you next. It hurts that you are so noncommittal when it seems we have a nice, easy flow." But I'd said nothing. I might have emailed him after our final date, telling him then what I told him two years later. Would that have short-circuited his meeting the geographically desirable woman? Past experience hadn't prepared me for this. In previous situations, if a man conversed with me warmly and enthusiastically, he liked me. If we spent three hours over dinner and a bottle of wine, talking animatedly, he liked me. If we hugged slowly and kissed intimately, he wanted the relationship to progress beyond kissing. But Brian held back, even with the enjoyable conversations and goodnight kisses.

I kept questioning how I had interpreted our flow—and questioning the questioning. Had Brian moved slowly because he had still been hung up on his deceased wife, even though he'd been widowed for a few years? Should I have been more outspoken, pushier? Had we both been self-protective, waiting for the other to say something? By our final date, however, it seemed clear that he wasn't interested in me. Regardless of what he said in his email, could he really be so clueless as not to know I liked him? I went from self-doubt to anger—there'd been a number of men who'd wanted to see more of me, but the feeling wasn't mutual. Then I finally met someone match-worthy, and he didn't share my sentiments. It was like being offered an occasional glass of wine when what I wanted was a magnum.

A few months later, my friend Marcia, a semiretired medical social worker, called. We'd met the previous year on a two-week tour to Cuba and had become close friends immediately as we probed the charms of the beautiful, shabby chic city of Havana, whose architecture, vegetation, and smells reminded me of New Orleans. She and her husband lived about a half-hour's drive from me. After returning to California, we met for hikes, lunches, and dinner. Marcia had reacted positively to my PASTRAMI pitch. Now she was suggesting I accompany her to a Saturday morning meditation class. She wanted me to meet the class leader, David, whose wife had died three years earlier of dementia; he had taken care of her during her illness and retired as a result of the caregiving demands. "Sallie, he's a fine human being, and he's smart as a whip—he was a Silicon Valley engineer. He seems like everything you're looking for—outgoing, yet introspective. Energetic and calm at the same time. Come see him run a session. But he doesn't know anything about your search. We'll have to figure out how to proceed if you like him."

I've taken meditation classes on at least five or six different occasions over the past thirty years. I'm not a natural at it, but I keep trying to improve. Emptying my mind of distractions, the goal of meditation, is a stretch. All kinds of thoughts clutter up my head: making a vet appointment, writing a thank-you note, going to the nursery to find out how to treat the white powdery mildew that's coating my roses, getting the tires rotated, and replacing the smoke alarm batteries.

And now I was going to a meditation session to check out a guy, under the pretense of wanting to inhale and exhale in a mindful way? On the one hand, it seemed anti-spiritual, but on the other, not so much. What if he turned out to be a soulful Eureka Man? (Sweet Pea: "Or, even if he doesn't, what if you became a passing-fair meditator?" Steve: "Like that's going to happen. Have you seen her mind lately?")

Marcia directed me to the meditation room and introduced me to David, who welcomed me with a handshake and a smile. "I hope you like it," he greeted me. Dressed in jeans, he was lean, with gray hair and a well-trimmed beard. Within minutes he told us to assume a comfortable position, either on the floor or on a chair. If seated on a chair, we were to uncross our legs and rest our hands on our laps, palms facing down. "Keep your back straight and your feet flat on the ground," he instructed softly. "And keep your eyes closed. Focus on your breathing. Be aware of each breath you take in and each one you let out." I sneaked a non-meditative peek at him to see if he had his eyes closed or was looking around, distracted and bored. His eyes were closed. "Breathe through your nose for four seconds, hold your breath for seven, and then breathe out for eight seconds, if you can. If you can't, do what you can. If it's hard to breathe out through your nose, exhale through your mouth. The important thing is to focus on your breathing."

I was thinking, "Hmmm . . . he's definitely a maybe, better than a maybe. Can't tell yet." I didn't know much about him, but I knew Marcia did. Plus there was nothing about him I didn't like. I peeked again and then a third time. He kept his eyes shut and appeared to be breathing in and out slowly.

He played soft music and spoke occasionally. "The music will help clear your mind of its chatter," he counseled. "Whenever you find your mind going back to your concerns, your worries, your to-do list, acknowledge it. Don't give up and don't scold yourself. It's natural to lose focus. Let it go and go back to breathing in and breathing out." The more he said, the more I liked David's calm demeanor and his way of balancing a straightforward approach with mindfulness. When I left, I felt his PASTRAMI potential ranked in the above-average to high category and looked forward to coming back in two Saturdays, the next time I'd be free.

Over the next week, I felt mutedly optimistic, but engaged in no chicken counting. I looked forward to getting to know him, although I had no idea how to let him know that I was available. I'm not an accomplished flirt, and Marcia and I were going to have to figure out how to proceed. But I didn't have to worry. Ten days later, Marcia emailed, "Well, damn. I'm sorry to say I went on his website, and he's posted a photo with his arm around a woman, announcing her as his new life partner. They're organizing a fall biking and meditation retreat in the Sierra. I gather you don't plan to sign up." Disappointed by the news, I nonetheless had to admit that a frequent peeker during meditation wasn't the ideal partner for Mr. Mindfulness, though for him I would have tried to empty my mind and breathe more deeply.

6

"TAKE IT TO THE LIMIT"

(The Eagles version,
but listen to Willie and Waylon too)

My low-tech way of approaching Love Liaisons for Candidate referrals wasn't going anywhere. Frustrated, I found myself wondering how to get PASTRAMI to go modestly viral—how to engage in a version of crowdfunding, with "funding" translating into PASTRAMI applicants, not dollars. Social media might, I told myself, be the answer, but I had no idea how to do it.

At Shawn's recommendation, I went to an online site called Upwork.com and reviewed resumés of a number of "technology producers" who'd posted their work histories and described consulting projects they'd worked on. I selected three individuals and emailed them, presenting PASTRAMI and asking how they'd put it in cyberspace. I wanted to get a sense of their creativity, flair, and working style, but most important was to find someone with a sense of humor. I chose a combination of writer, strategist, and social media expert whose positive response and enthusiasm won me over. Matthew worked out of his house in Los Angeles. He was forty and married; his wife was pregnant with their first child, a baby girl.

Knowing he'd studied the PASTRAMI website, I wondered if he saw me as desperate and pathetic. He said nothing to indicate he saw it as a lonely hearts project, but simply made a few suggestions for streamlining the text. When he asked about one of the photos, his voice filled with admiration, "You really let a tarantula crawl up your arm in Costa Rica?" I knew we were all right. The rest of our conversation focused on how to simplify the application process for Candidates.

Matthew's next recommendation was to link my personal Facebook page to a PASTRAMI page or ad, making use of my existing network of friends, and, by extension, my friends' networks and their friends' networks.

"Matthew, I can't do that. It's not comfortable. I'd be humiliated." I sounded exactly like I had when my friend Russ suggested I place an ad in the *Bay Guardian*. But back then the ad was anonymous. Now my name and search details would be blasted out to my friends, Keith, my ex-husband, and the occasional man at Rotary I'd rebuffed by saying I was involved with someone.

But Matthew was firm. "It doesn't make sense to keep your search under the radar. That's why dating sites exist—so you can reach the right people and be discreet at the same time."

Still, I refused his suggestion to link my Facebook page to a PASTRAMI ad, so we went with his backup plan: placing four ten-day PASTRAMI ads on Facebook in metropolitan Washington, DC, where my sister and nephew live, and in the San Francisco Bay Area—one for Candidates and one for Love Liaisons in each location. The ad for Candidates targeted single males sixty-five and older, who spoke English, had similar interests to mine, were college graduates, and liked women.

Any hope I had that his Plan B social media experiment would pull in a fair number of demographically desirable men was short-lived. In the DC area, nearly three thousand men looked at the ad, over a hundred visited the Project PASTRAMI.com site (a 3.7 percent click rate, at least higher than the average one percent), but I received zero emails. In the Bay Area, over thirty-three hundred men viewed the ad, around a hundred fifty visited my site, and one man wrote me. He was a recent widower in his mid-eighties who lived several hours away; he was in deep mourning after his wife's long-term illness just months earlier. I wrote him back, thanked him, offered my condolences, and said I was seeking someone who lived closer by, but in truth I didn't think he was ready. Plus I didn't warm to the age difference, actuarially speaking.

The effort to attract Love Liaisons was equally unsuccessful, but Matthew had prepared me for that from the start. We had scratched our heads about how to proceed and ultimately decided, seat-of-the-pants style, to target females age forty and over, with the same qualities and interests as the Candidates. "This one is tricky," Matthew warned me. "Here, you're targeting the person who knows the person. Social media doesn't work like that." He was right—out of a total of 10,663 views in the two geographical areas, only 130 potential Love Liaisons visited PASTRAMI, and not one sent an email referring a Candidate. To his credit, Matthew didn't make me feel worse by saying, "I told you so." (Steve: "I'll say it. He told you so." Sweet Pea: "Be quiet. She feels bad enough already.")

Following the lackluster Facebook ad results, I went into a PASTRAMI slump: I stopped giving my sassy pitch to the potential Love Liaisons remaining on my list. I didn't add new names to the list or think of other ways to promote my search. I didn't connect with Tina and Shawn to ask them to give me a boost. And I didn't keep my sister apprised of progress because there wasn't any. Virginia, however, caught on. She had a two-day business conference scheduled in San Francisco and called to announce she wanted to spend an extra week with me so she could run charismatizing sessions. "Sallie, I want to meet your Love Liaisons. Let's make sure they stay energized." She also wanted to hear my PASTRAMI pitch and help tweak it. "And let's strategize ways to market PASTRAMI to a wider audience."

I invited first Shawn and then Tina to go out to eat with Virginia and me, so we could pick their brains. Over dinner at a nearby favorite restaurant, Shawn gave me names of Berkeley Rotarians he thought I should approach, a few of whom I hadn't put on my list. He reviewed those I'd already contacted and suggested I refresh some of those contacts. "Remind them. It can't hurt. Plus, you know about Robert Bly's Mankind Project?" Virginia and I both were aware of the movement that encourages men to explore their innermost feelings in group and retreat settings. "Well, find out how they market, and market to that group. They're in your age and educational demographics. They're just what you're looking for. So is REI's market. Find out how to reach them." Shawn's ideas sounded good to me. I had no sense of how to do this but figured Matthew would know.

Several days before my sister's departure, I couldn't put my pitch demo off any more. I launched into my spiel with my eyes connecting with hers and our sisterly vibes flowing.

"Hey, Gin," I began. "I need your help. I'm on a manhunt and want you to be a Love Liaison for me."

Playing along as an unsuspecting friend, she said, "How so?"

"I have a process I call PASTRAMI—here's a handout about it—each letter in PASTRAMI stands for a quality I want my hunka' hunka' burning love to have. P is for the physical part. A is for adventurous and also animal lover. S stands for spiritual. It goes on, with an M for monkey business, and I for intellectual. Yes, I want it all."

Gin was grinning ear to ear and laughing.

I hastened to add, "And there's a five-thousand-dollar donation to a nonprofit if you help me find him and we become partners."

I delivered my pitch smoothly, self-confidently, saucily. The cherry on top was handing over the hot pink envelope. "There's lots more on my PASTRAMI website."

"Sallie, what's the problem?" she asked after I'd finished. "You've nailed it. Why do you say you can't do it?"

"Gin, that was easy. You were with me all the way."

"Why wouldn't your friends be with you too? Don't let stodgy people hold you back."

Virginia and I also brainstormed ways to market my quest. Among the proposed approaches I considered was to identify a UC Berkeley professor in the Sociology or Psychology Department, someone specializing in gerontology. Such a person might have novel ideas about networking with specific communities (men's groups, senior hiking clubs, and retiree groups). We considered the possibility of a graduate student using PASTRAMI for a thesis or a dissertation to explore issues around senior love, senior loneliness, and senior mental health. "How about rejoining one or more of the online sites you quit?" Virginia suggested. "You could embed PASTRAMI in it." I agreed that made sense, but I cringed at the prospect of more dead ends. "Along with a brief profile and photo or two, just direct men to Project PASTRAMI for an in-depth description of what you're seeking."

Virginia was also big on my identifying professional groups who could refer me to potential Candidates. "Financial planners and estate lawyers are good bets," she pointed out. "And hair stylists and restaurant managers. And funeral parlor directors."

"Why don't I read the obituaries for women who've died recently?" Seeing her eyes light up with amusement, I continued, "Then, if she's survived by a husband who appears to be in my age bracket, I could attend the funeral and check him out." By now we had crumpled into giggles. The sisterly irreverence continued, "Then six months from now, out of the blue, I'll hang outside his house and bump into him accidentally on purpose. Yes?"

Virginia pretended to be considering the idea. "Or read obits from last year and figure out how to run into them now. Ideally they'd be ready and you wouldn't have to wait. Or, better yet, make the rounds of funeral directors and ask them to introduce you. Mention the finder's fee."

In spite of our amusement, we acknowledged, unspoken, the sadness inherent in the topics of death, mourning, and the hope of starting a new life. I was both encouraged and apprehensive. How much was I willing to push the edges of the box I found myself in? Or break down the box to get what I wanted?

A short time later, I had an appointment with my dermatologist. I've been going to Dori for more than ten years, and we're on a first name basis. Pretty, slim, and fashionable, even under her white physician's coat, Dori is a model for what a woman in her mid-fifties would want to look like. She has a short, bouncy blondish gray bob, lively hazel eyes, and a playful smile. Most of Dori's patients have some form of skin cancer, while my condition—rosacea and the occasional broken capillaries and brown spots—is cosmetic rather than medical.

I had no intention of telling her about PASTRAMI. She was my doctor, not my confidante. But on the spur of the moment, I pulled an envelope out of my purse and launched into PASTRAMI. "I'm on the hunt for a man and want to give you this. I'd love your help, your thoughts."

"But aren't you going with the retired professor?" she asked, recalling the Almost Enough man. After I filled her in on the breakup, she went into problem-solving mode. "I think you should go on college-sponsored foreign tours. I know you love to travel." During the ten minutes we'd been talking PASTRAMI, her assistant had buzzed twice to tell her she was late for the next patient. "Coming," Dori responded the second time, then started down the hall toward the other exam room. When she was halfway there, she suddenly swiveled to face me again. "Oh, I hate going back to work. This has been fun," she laughed. "I need to think more about this!" As she entered the new examining room, she called out to her assistant, "This visit's free for Sallie. We didn't do a treatment. We had fun."

7

"SOMEWHERE BEYOND THE SEA"

(Yes, Bobby Darin—and he wrote it—
but the We Five version is great too)

In mid-February of 2017, in recognition of Valentine's Day and my seventy-third birthday the following day, I forced myself to reactivate PASTRAMI and contacted more potential matchmakers on my list. It was my birthday present to myself, a toast to the heartening prospect of love at any age. By early summer I'd enlisted twenty more Love Liaisons, bringing the total to fifty-four.

Shawn introduced me to a guy named Glen, a Berkeley hippie for years. When he was in his late thirties, he'd given up his tie-dye life and started a small business that grew into a community treasure supporting local nonprofits. I went out with Glen a couple of times, but we didn't move to the next step because he reminded me of Matt in disconcerting ways. His deep voice was similar to Matt's, as was his street-savvy way of talking. I felt like Lauren Bacall, whose second husband, Jason Robards, must have seemed like a diluted version of her first husband, Humphrey Bogart. (Steve: "Great. Her friend introduces her to someone he thinks is special and she shoots herself in the foot. Ding—she loses." Sweet Pea: "There was no ding. She's waiting for the bells.")

Another dear Rotarian, John, introduced me to Toby, a high school teacher/educator/part-time Stanford instructor of education. I liked Toby a lot. We talked about books and theater, and we cohosted at least three dinner parties with his friends. He wasn't as drawn to me as I was to him—conversations and dinners with his colleagues were the starting and stopping points of our dates. To my dismay, we never moved beyond that point, other than for me to meet him at a shoe store that specialized in orthopedic inserts. The store did not accept new customers without a personal introduction (mine) or a referral from a podiatrist, and I was happy to provide that introduction, but would have preferred a candlelit dinner for two.

Rotarian friend Judith took me to a social event at a private club she and her husband belonged to. She subtly, but pointedly, introduced me to a few single men, who had no knowledge of PASTRAMI. Again, no bites.

My friend Shawn, always in my corner, stepped up for a second time. "Sallie, I know a guy you might like. I don't know Ross all that well, but I think he might just be the guy." I asked Shawn to tell me more. "He's a retired architect from Reno and comes down to the Bay Area all the time to sail. He keeps his boat here. I can't speak to all the PASTRAMI qualities, but I can vouch that he's bright, fit, energetic, and available. Why don't I talk with him?"

Shawn called his friend, who responded in the affirmative. The next day sailor Ross emailed me, providing personal tidbits that Shawn hadn't known (divorced five years, three kids, four grandchildren for starters) and added, "I'm up for the adventure!" He invited me to meet him that Friday at three o'clock at Brickyard Cove in Richmond. We'd go sailing, watch the sun descend over the Bay, and have dinner at the Richmond Yacht Club. I texted Shawn about the upcoming date, and he responded in his irrepressibly upbeat fashion: "If he doesn't fall for you in the first five minutes, he's not the man I think he is."

I tried not to be optimistic, but I was. I counted the days and then the hours till Friday afternoon. When I got in my car to drive the twenty minutes to meet Ross, I wondered how it would feel to care for someone again. To make a connection again. Not to be lonely. (Steve: "Here we go again, getting our hopes up." Sweet Pea: "She wants a birthday present, and this could be it.").

When Ross met me at the locked gate to the dock at the Richmond Marina, I liked what I saw. Tanned, tall, and dressed in jeans, a navy T-shirt and white tennis shoes, he greeted me in an easy, friendly manner. We walked along the wooden walkway to slip forty-two, where his twenty-nine-foot white-and-blue Catalina was tied to the dock. Jumping into the cockpit with the bounce of an eighteen-year-old, he extended his hand to this cautious landlubber. "Come aboard," he urged. I took his hand, but, starting to trip, I caught the lifeline with my other hand. (Steve: "So not cool." Sweet Pea: "Maybe he didn't notice." Steve: "He noticed.")

"Ross," I admitted, "I know very little about sailing. I want to help. But keep it simple." Maybe I should have told him that my sailing skills consist of remembering which side is starboard and which is port, which end of the boat is the bow and which is the stern, and knowing how to secure my life jacket. I also have a lot of experience going down the stairs into the galley, retrieving cold beer and wine from the refrigerator, and climbing back up the stairs to distribute drinks to those on deck. Another thing I neglected to tell him was that, from painful experience, I knew what it meant when someone says, "Watch out for the boom."

"Sure," Ross responded. "You can help me take the cover off the mains'l and fold it." At least somehow I knew "s'l" meant "sail." He'd already begun removing the cover, and I pitched in, trying to fold my end as tightly as his. He suggested I secure the gate, but I looked around and didn't see a gate. So he did it himself, attaching a loose wire (that would be the gate) with a hook (actually a pelican hook, he informed me) to the stanchion (a post). Next he wanted me to cast off the dock lines. I followed his line of sight, hoping to figure out what he was looking at. I wished he'd point—anything to give me a hint of what nautical maneuver to undertake. "I'm sorry. I have no idea what you're talking about." Accustomed to being competent and helpful, I hated my inability to assist this sailing super-aficionado.

After Ross detached, jiggered, and toggled, we motored out of the slip, away from the dock, and into the fairway. "Can you steer while I raise the mains'l?" he inquired. Sensing my hesitation, he added, "Just steer into the wind. It's like steering a car. You can control the furling line while we deploy the jib."

"Deploy?" I thought to myself. "We?" Saying nothing, I took the wheel, figuring he'd stop me if he saw us heading for disaster. Ross continued with something about unfurling the jib and rolling the furling or furling the roller. I was bewildered. In time, he stopped asking and took over all the operations, adjusting the sails and lines by himself.

With the pulling and furling behind him, Ross settled on a course. As I was making small talk about how pretty the Bay was in the late afternoon, he said, "I leave in a few weeks for Europe with some friends. We'll be sailing for two months in the Mediterranean."

"Oh, wow! You really love sailing, eh?" I said, hoping I didn't sound as deflated as I felt. I was clearly not the sailing partner he sought, and I didn't share his fervor for the wind and water enough to want to learn to be. This wasn't going anywhere, and I just wanted to get through the rest of the day and be back on solid ground.

"Yep. And I'm starting to do land sailing too, so I can sail all year long."

"Land sailing?" This guy was more besotted with sailing than I had imagined.

"Think of it as bicycling on three or four wheels with a sail and speeding through the desert, often in salt flats," he responded enthusiastically. "People call it sand sailing and land yachting too. So far I've land sailed outside of Las Vegas and in Southern California. I'm going back to Vegas after I return from the Mediterranean, and next year some friends and I are going to Aruba. They tell me it's fabulous for land sailing."

As we continued sailing around San Pablo Bay, he explained how the winds and the weather affected decisions about which sail or line to pull, push, loosen, or tighten. I nodded and asked a few questions, struggling to understand his explanations. To my disappointment, but not surprise, he asked nothing about my activities, interests, or background—the conversation was about sailing and nothing but sailing. After a while—but not soon enough—we turned south toward the harbor, setting our course back to the marina, where I helped, as best I could, flake the main, furl the jib, cover the mainsail (my standout contribution), put the fenders out, and tie down his boat. I could have been a robot for all the interest Ross showed in me as we prepared to leave the boat, although a robot would have flaked and furled more competently than I had.

At dinner we shared a table with four people Ross knew. After everyone ordered, conversation focused on sailing. To my relief, our table companions introduced themselves and asked me where I was from and what I did. They inquired about my life in Berkeley and listened as I talked about my volunteer work and medical interpreting in Central America. But Ross never did. For him, it was sailing and sailing and then, not surprisingly, more sailing. For me it was about drinking the first glass of wine, then finding someone on the waitstaff to bring me a second one. We skipped dessert and coffee, for which I was grateful.

After dinner, Ross walked me to the parking area. He said good-bye without mentioning a next time.

Driving home, I let my dashed hopes morph into a more positive reaction: I hadn't been rejected by Ross. We were simply incompatible species. He was a marine mammal and I was a terrestrial.

I pulled into my driveway, got out of the car, and sighed with relief at my front yard, with the roses, rosemary bushes, and geranium-filled flower box bathed in the street light. "Give me this any day," I thought. "I choose dirt and trees and sidewalks over sails, cockpits, and lifelines. And walking, gardening, and picking up dog poop."

But I couldn't help feeling a little discouraged. When had dating become so hard?

8

"MANY RIVERS TO CROSS"

(Jimmy Cliff version)

In my late teens and early twenties, I met and dated boys and young men I knew in high school and college. Male friends were abundant, boyfriends less so, but still around. And I had another way to meet potential mates: In New Orleans, where my family moved as I started my senior year of high school, a tradition of "please escorts" had evolved among the Uptown gentry. When an unmarried *jeune fille* was invited to a debutante party (with the invitation often addressed in calligraphy to the *mademoiselle*—in my case to Mlle. Sallie Weissinger), she received an announcement indicating the name of the eligible gentleman who'd escort her to the event. She might or might not know the gentleman, but she would likely recognize the family name. He might even end up becoming a husband for the marriageable young lady.

In my case, none of my "please escorts" was someone I wanted to date beyond the single choreographed evening, but each escort was good company and invariably performed his duties with gentlemanly aplomb: opening the door for me, helping me on and off with my coat, making sure I was never alone. And, of course, he'd move my chair to seat me if we'd danced, whether I required assistance or not. He invariably looked smart in his tuxedo or tails and displayed impeccable social skills. "May I get you a drink?" an escort would invariably ask before heading for the bar. "What would you like?"

I hadn't the slightest idea what any of the drinks, poured so liberally in New Orleans, tasted like, so I would ask, "What are you drinking?" No matter what he responded, I'd say, "Oh, I like that. Thanks."

My sister and I called these young men "debutantes' delights," DDs for short, a term we made sure our mother did not overhear. A dyed-in-the-wool daughter of New Orleans, Mom was ever hopeful we would be more excited about our DD adventures than we were. Having been raised in non-Deep South parts, Virginia and I found the tradition of debutante parties and fancy Mardi Gras balls magical and fascinating, more theater than real life.

However sophisticated our New Orleans environment was, neither of us was comfortable in the DD ambience. My mother wanted me to "come out" in society at that prescribed time in my social development, but even a watered-down version of a debut would have been more than my parents could afford. I would have to glide around the dance floor in a ball gown two sizes larger than any of my more slender classmates were wearing. And I would have to learn to make small talk and figure out what drink to order. All this was avoided when I chose to study in Spain my junior year of college.

I received a partial scholarship and took out a loan to pay the balance of my tuition and fees for my year abroad at the University of Madrid. I covered travel expenses by tutoring high school students in Spanish and math and by proctoring Spanish in the university language lab. My parents sent me a hundred dollars a month for spending money and, whenever possible, a little extra. They were strapped for money, saving to buy a house after my father's retirement. My mother had gone back to work after being out of the job market for more than twenty years.

For the first time, I was truly living away from home. I shared a room in a Spanish dorm with two young Spanish women who took me under their sisterly wings. Although I was often homesick, especially at Christmas, I was jazzed at the prospect of being on my own and honing my Spanish language skills.

After Spain, I went to graduate school in Berkeley for two years and then married a fellow military brat from Indiana (that would be Daniel) at age twenty-two, got divorced at twenty-nine, and moved with three-year-old Heather to California. In my thirties, I chose a forever life with Matt, a first-generation American, whose parents were born in Ukraine and Poland. The social skills I had picked up along the way, sad to say, had not prepared me for the subsequent drama of conducting an online partner search.

Apart from the two training-wheel adventures, during my dozen pre-PASTRAMI years of Internet dating, I identified five discrete categories of men: first, the quirky man I loved but not enough; second, the two others who stood out: Brian, who didn't return my affections, and Stan, whose wife's beauty evidently still lured him; third, the cohort of perfectly nice men I dated short-term to make sure I was giving us a chance; and fourth, the hundred-plus men who never went beyond the coffee phase. Then there is the fifth and final category: memorable encounters with soap opera overtones. Fortunately for my self-esteem, I met these Category Five men, including the two gold diggers, during my last eighteen months of online dating. By then I was better at handling disappointments and, for the most part, viewed them as juicy misadventures that would make great stories.

There was Michael, a financial investment manager with a bookish side. He was physically fit and energetic, although his feisty streetwise edge made me a bit uncomfortable. We weren't a long-term match, but at least I was having fun for a change. We drove down to Half Moon Bay to buy salmon straight from the fishing boats and cooked it at my house. We went to dinner with my friends. I introduced him to my sister when she visited. Michael knew a lot about gardening, and he replanted and fertilized three of my drooping front yard plants. We sat on the floor in my den, listening to rock and roll music. After eight or ten dates in a six-week period, when I Googled him to see if he was on Facebook or LinkedIn, I found newspaper articles summarizing a court case in which he was accused of misappropriating firm funds. He had repaid the money within a few weeks, before the auditors identified the crime. He was spared a jail sentence, but left the firm and the field. When I told him what I'd found, he confirmed the accuracy of the articles. "I planned to tell you," he said, "but didn't know how and when to do it." I believed Michael but couldn't get past what he'd done. I wrote him that I didn't feel we had a future. His response was lovely: "That was a courageous message you sent me. Thank you for being honest in all respects. It was not unexpected, however. I surmised that, if you felt as I believed you would, I'd hear from you. It's ironic that I finally found the person who has the characteristics I seek, and yet, I didn't measure up. And I knew I didn't." He ended by wishing me all the luck in the world and said he was glad we'd met.

Five months later, Miles appeared on the horizon. I found him attractive, charismatic, and well-spoken. During our spirited caffeinated conversation, I didn't check my watch once. He lived in the North Bay and worked as a management consultant in Sacramento. Shortly after our meeting, I left for New Orleans to visit family and friends. While I was away, Miles flew to the Midwest to visit his daughter, a single mother-to-be. He'd arranged his work schedule to be with her during labor and help during her first week at home with the baby. We emailed most days.

Once again a promising glow peeked through the dating shadows. But after the string of disappointments, I decided to check Miles on the Internet and see if he was on Facebook. I found much more than I'd bargained for: newspaper accounts from ten years earlier of a child molestation judgment, which he had not contested. It was not the first incident. I emailed him that "I was totally surprised—in fact, stunned—to see the write-up on the legal case involving you. I have no idea how to react—unless there's a huge mistake. Is that you?"

"There is no mistake," he replied swiftly. "I have a history. If that is a deal breaker for you, let me know."

It was.

For a person who doesn't feed on high drama, these incidents out of a *telenovela* should have led me to quit—not just the online dating, but the whole search for a mate. Still, in spite of the unsavory outcomes, I maintained an inner resolve not to let the seediness bring me down. "This has to be as bad as it will get," I told myself. "I'm gonna get a break." I continued to believe in something good happening after the bad.

And yet within the year, there were two more unsavory episodes. The first involved a semiretired lawyer from Marin whose profile presented an accomplished, engaging man. He wrote well, displaying a wry sense of tongue-in-cheek humor. Shortly after meeting at a restaurant during happy hour, he began touching my arm and shoulder and trying to kiss me. "Please stop doing that," I requested. But he kept grabbing. "I asked you to stop," I repeated futilely, my voice getting louder. I set down a twenty-dollar bill for the glass of wine I had barely begun to sip and started to leave.

"Bitch," he yelled at me as I got up. "You're a bitch." Diners put down their forks and stared as he continued yelling and I walked out. I wasn't frightened or angry as I left the restaurant, just disgusted and bone-weary of the bullshit. I was home in five minutes and poured myself a welcome glass of wine.

My coffee with a former college professor who worked part-time as a landscaper went well enough to merit a follow-up meeting. He seemed articulate, serious, and pleasant. When he invited me to take a hike in the hills near his home, I was happy to accept. The plan was to meet at his house. As I walked toward his front porch, a jumble of two broken-down barbecues and assorted pieces of unidentifiable rusty equipment, possibly tractor parts, by the front door greeted me. I double-checked the address, which matched what he'd written on the card I held. Inside, eight bicycles and countless bike parts and tools filled his living room; unopened boxes and stacks of books covered the dining room table and kitchen counters. There was no empty chair on which to sit down in this hoarder's abode. Driving home after the hike, I took a deep, slow breath and thought, "No more junk in my life."

I launched into yet another bout of self-criticism. As a confirmed feminist, I've taken care of myself financially since my graduate school days; no man, including Matt, ever worked to support me. I've competed professionally with men and often outperformed them. I've carved out a life for myself as an independent person, even when happily married, and refused to settle for less than a hundred percent.

This sixties feminist cringes to admit it, but she will nonetheless: I still carried in my heart the dream of having butterflies fluttering in my body one more time. I wanted someone with me in the lonely places—the places I had walked through alone until Matt showed up—and I wanted equally much to fill someone else's lonely places. Two people occupying each other's lonely places, through affection, humor, conversation, passion, and whatever else gets them through hard times end up not being lonely after all. Showering. Pruning roses. Cleaning out the refrigerator.

But—and this time it was a major *but*—after years of hitting dead end after dead end, I'd had it. I couldn't face another caffeinated hour like the ones I'd been gritting my teeth to get through. I terminated my two online memberships. I was done with online dating sites populated by liars, cheats, child molesters, scam artists, lesser toads and frogs, and the innocuous guys who offered nothing wrong but nothing right. I threw in the e-dating towel.

Maybe Matt was the last man I would love. Maybe it all ended when Matt died.

9

"RING OF FIRE"

(Johnny Cash version—
because what else is there?)

Within a few months of meeting at Ortman's in 1978, Matt and I were living together in my house, although he sublet his studio apartment in south Berkeley for a couple of years. Bruised by his first marriage, he wanted an escape route in case we didn't make it.

When we began going together to the Berkeley Unitarian Church, movies, plays, concerts, farmers markets, and crafts fairs, we found ourselves saying hello to the same people. "How do you know Debra?" I asked one evening after he said hello to her in the Safeway parking lot.

"We've worked together on a couple of church presentations over the past several years," he told me.

"She and I have been in the church women's group for two years, and I've talked about wanting to meet a man," I told him as we loaded grocery bags into the back of his Subaru hatchback.

"Well, she's hinted a couple of times she'd like us to go out," he replied sheepishly. "And I've ignored the signals."

We wondered why we hadn't connected through traditional channels. We'd attended the same church off and on for years, sticking around for the fellowship hour after the Sunday morning sermon and going to evening potlucks and occasional concerts. We had friends in common who knew each of us was single. Not long after we started seeing each other, he announced to the other eight members of his men's group, "I've met a woman from Louisiana. I think I'm falling for her."

"Sallie Weissinger?" one of them asked.

It frightened me to think how huge a role chance had played in altering my life. Our fates had been transformed because he picked up a newspaper on a certain day and happened to turn to a specific page, where he saw my brief ad, which ran only twice. Four times every weekend he'd passed half a block from my house, as he drove to and from Marin County on Friday nights and again on Sunday evenings to pick up his daughters and take them home again. Scores of times I must have been in my front yard, chatting with a neighbor on the sidewalk or kneeling in the garden, as, without my knowing it, the great love-to-be of my life passed a few hundred yards away.

Or what if he hadn't asked for his photo back? After I met Matt and reread his letter, I didn't understand—and still don't—why I placed him in the MAYBE pile. He was incredulous about his near fate, "You put me in the maybe pile of life?" He repeated that phrase for years, laughingly telling our families and friends, "Can you believe it? I should have been a resounding YES, but she dumped me in the maybe pile of life!"

Matt and I couldn't have been more different. At the age he was playing stickball and then baseball with his buddies on

Eastern Parkway in Brooklyn, I was training to be an Uptown lady, learning to set a formal table, writing thank-you notes, and going to dinner parties and teas in New Orleans. His parents, both born in Eastern Europe, spoke Yiddish as well as English. His father left school after fifth grade, and his mother completed eighth grade. Both my parents had college degrees. While Matt spent his entire childhood in one neighborhood, my father's military career took us to Germany and Japan, as well as numerous places in the States, primarily in the Midwest.

Our twelve-year age difference seemed unimportant, given his activity level. He did a hundred push-ups a day and introduced me to the exhilarating pleasure of taking twenty-five-mile bike rides in Sonoma and Napa. He taught me, a city girl, to camp and backpack in the Sierra, an embarrassing learning experience because his two younger preteen daughters, Sally and Claire, could carry heavier packs than I could and were hardier on the trails than I was. They taught me how to navigate streams without falling and encouraged me to keep going when I was lagging behind. They also taught me to pee in the woods, facing downhill, and away from the wind.

Everything about Matt, especially his life force and brash self-confidence, excited me, though it took a while to get accustomed to the level of noise he generated. Matt operated at high speed and high decibels. In addition to his booming voice, music was always playing on the radio, television, or combination record-cassette player—Ella Fitzgerald, George Gershwin, Willie Nelson, the Beatles, and sixties folk music. Regardless of which room in the house he occupied—he'd be futzing in the back as I walked in the front door—the noise level told me where he was.

While I'm far from being a sports fan, I loved hearing Matt talk about his boyhood addiction to his beloved Brooklyn

Dodgers. He reminisced about how he and his pals used to take their pillows and blankets to Ebbets Field after dark and sleep on the ground outside the stadium so they could buy cheap tickets when the box office opened in the morning. When he talked about "the Bums," he was a little kid worshipping his heroes, Pee Wee Reese and Jackie Robinson in particular. He had refused to sign a petition to boycott the team if the Dodgers signed Robinson. And he never forgave them for moving to Los Angeles.

Matt's focus on the human side of baseball underscored his lifelong commitment to treating people of different ethnic groups fairly. He'd been on the receiving end of discrimination himself. When he was at Columbia on a full scholarship, he was invited by Sigma Chi Fraternity to join their ranks. "I didn't particularly want to join a Greek fraternity and I didn't go out for rush, but they were a good group of guys. I was going to accept—until I found out they'd invited me to be their token Jew. I didn't look Jewish and my name wasn't Goldberg or Stein, so they could have it both ways: get credit for having taken in a Jew without it being obvious. Screw 'em. I said no."

Of course, he wasn't perfect. Far from it. He could be abrasive in interactions with people and curt, even insulting, to coworkers. One day he came home furious that Susan, the office secretary, hadn't followed his instructions to photocopy and collate a number of binders for an annual training conference for new trial judges. Since he was still fuming hours later, I was pretty sure he had reduced Susan to tears. I suggested that next time he should ask her to repeat his instructions, and he should check her work well before she was finished so she could fix any glitches. Most important, he should keep his voice down. "There's no reason to yell and scare people." Matt seemed genuinely surprised by that—yelling? That was just the way he talked. He took my words seriously and seemed chastened. In time, when I visited him at work, Susan and some of the other support staff approached me, whispering confidentially, "Sallie, I don't know what you've done, but Matt has gotten much nicer."

But there were times when even he acknowledged he was at a high-voltage yelling level. He would lose his temper during phone calls with his ex-wife and run-ins with my increasingly snippy preteen daughter. Rude car drivers and oblivious bicyclists speeding through stop signs were a source of fury. A frustrating wait in line at the bagel store could catapult him to a ten on the raging-bull scale, with me as the recipient of his ire. He'd yell, get it off his chest, and forget it.

I was the opposite. Once my feelings were hurt, I held on to my resentment like a child clinging to a teddy bear. Because I hadn't learned to stand up for myself with my obey-me-or-else Air Force colonel of a father or my New Orleans be-a-lady-at-all-times mother, it took a while to put Matt's outbursts in perspective. They were rarely aimed at me anyway. Sometimes I'd put my hand on his knee and just say, "Hey, Matt, it's okay. Sweetheart, calm down." At other times, I had to remind him, "Hey, dammit, I am not the enemy. I'm the one who loves you. Stop yelling." And he did, usually immediately.

Once I was able to counter his anger without melting down, Matt asked me, "Why are you so nice to everyone else and so impatient with me? Why don't you put up with any shit from me, when I see you taking it at work and from friends?"

"Because you would steamroll over me if I didn't speak up, and where would that leave us?" I responded with a knowing smile. "I have to keep you from overwhelming me because I love you."

He pondered for a moment. "You're right. I wish I were calmer, but you know what? I'm good for you too. I give you a sharper edge. You're better off with me than with those stuffy New Orleans WASPs your mother wanted you to marry." Then he paid me the highest possible compliment, "Sarah, you have never bored me. Not for one minute. You've perplexed me, you've pissed me off, but you've never bored me."

I felt the same. Throughout the ups and downs, we had friendship, humor, chemistry, and a limitless supply of good will going for us. Cooking and eating dinner together, whether we dished up something simple or my three-star jambalaya, was a special occasion. On work nights we'd throw leftovers together, with weekends reserved for culinary experiments. "Tell me what to do," he'd offer, volunteering his *sous-chef* services, chopping, stirring, and tasting, as well as cleaning up afterward. He watched me bustle around and wondered out loud, "How can you do everything else while I'm still chopping?" He didn't consider it was because, in between chopping and mincing, he'd been in the den, searching for the next Frank and Ella selections, and reading me anecdotes from the liner notes.

If we read about a big band event in the city, we got dressed up to go waltzing and fox-trotting in San Francisco. Matt would proudly put on his threadbare college tux, which still fit him comfortably. I'd don my opera outfit: a slinky silver top, clingy black palazzo pants, and open-toed, ankle-strap high heels. I was grateful for my mother's insistence that, as a preteen, I take Arthur Murray ballroom dancing lessons. We danced in the kitchen many nights as we cooked and in the street if the mood struck us. One Monday morning at the office, a coworker said she'd seen someone who looked like me in downtown Berkeley, dancing across four lanes of cars that were waiting for a red light to change. "But I was probably wrong," she added. She wasn't. I admitted we were the culprits. I didn't tell her we were also singing as we glided across Shattuck Avenue, pretending to be Fred Astaire and Ginger Rogers.

Always an actor, Matt imitated foreign or regional accents whenever the urge struck him. When I was away from my office, and my secretary would answer my phone, Matt often identified himself in a crisp, upper-class British accent as John Brailsford, a London solicitor. Sometimes a western-twanged cowboy named Bat Guano called from Nevada. Other times I had messages from a crusty-voiced Armando Ferrucci, echoing Marlon Brando's Sicilian godfather. My secretary never asked who these men with foreign accents were or why they called so often. I wondered if she thought I was having multiple affairs.

Changing his accent came easy. He'd wanted to be a stage actor, but, when his mother was outraged at the prospect of a son without a viable profession, Matt chose the law as a distant second choice. Nevertheless, he continued pouring his enthusiasm for the stage into acting in community theater, one of his many hobbies. Matt could swing into a remarkable version of Charlie Chaplin's little tramp or Gene Kelly twirling his umbrella and singing in the rain.

When he played the bus driver in *Bus Stop*, a romantic comedy-drama, Matt invented another role for himself, this time both inside and outside the theater. For a few weeks at the Point Richmond Masquers, an intimate community theater north of Berkeley, he appeared on stage during Acts I and III, but during Act II he was free to wander. Staying in his bus driver's uniform, he strolled several doors down to a bar, where he drank a ginger ale and chatted, in character, with the bartender. The bartender talked primarily about how the 49ers were doing and a bit about his family, while Matt discussed how many passengers he'd picked up on his Greyhound bus route from Sacramento to San Jose. He complained about the increased traffic, an annoying passenger, the fog causing a slowdown, and an occasional accident on the freeway. On closing night, Matt told the bartender he'd be gone a while, since the company had reassigned him to cover a route in Southern California.

Ten years after we met, he achieved a lifelong goal: he got to play Nathan Detroit in *Guys and Dolls* at Piedmont Light Civic Opera. The write-up in the local paper praised his Runyonesque portrayal as humorous and powerful, adding he stole the show with "the perfect portrait of a grizzled gambler with a soft spot for a classy doll."

His acting was not limited to the stage. Matt played one of his best tricks in the bathroom adjacent to our bedroom. Not having grown up with brothers, I was fascinated by how a man urinates standing, and I often commented, with a note of resentment, about the fact that men have it easier than women in that arena. It was annoying how quickly he could pee and be done with it. One evening, however, he took far longer than usual—he peed and peed and peed, somewhat noisily, with the door open. As he came to bed, I commented, "Matt-a-Muffin (my pet name for him), that went on forever. Did you drink a gallon of water or what?" His eyes glittered with amusement as he confessed, "I knew you'd be listening, Ms. Nosy, so I took the big watering can from the garden into the bathroom with me and poured it into the toilet as slowly as I could. That'll teach you."

It wasn't unusual for us, especially on weekends, to wake each other up at two in the morning, to share our dreams and fall back to sleep. "I dreamt I came home and called for you," he once said, waking me in the early morning semi-darkness.

"I couldn't find you but knew you were in the backyard. I opened the back door, still calling, and saw you behind a tree at the back fence, not answering. I asked why you were hiding from me." His voice was tinged with concern and he was staring at me with a serious look on his face. He then asked why I'd been distant and sexually diminished the last several weeks. He was aware that, since I'd been promoted at work, I was both learning my new job and doing my old job until someone could be hired to replace me.

"I'm on overload, trying to do everything," I said apologetically as I put my hand on his arm. "It's like running for a train and almost catching it over and over. It speeds up just as I think I can catch it. But it keeps moving faster, and I can't go any faster. I'm exhausted."

"Well, then tell me that. You act like everything's under control. You don't seem upset or especially tired, but you go underground on me. You dwindle. And I'm left guessing whether we're okay. Are we?"

"We are more than okay," I assured him, putting my head on his chest. "You are what makes it all worth it. I'm shitty at keeping work in perspective. Knowing I have us to come home to is what keeps me going."

And then he said what he often did, "Sarah, give yourself a break. You bust your ass and think you should be able to do more. They don't deserve that much of you." Well, that's not exactly all he said. He added a Matt-ism: "Sarah, fuck 'em. They don't get all of you. I don't suck hind tit."

It was an intellectual intimacy I had never experienced as an adult, mixed with the trust of a child, which I had felt with my parents. I knew he wouldn't hold back or cover up his feelings, and I didn't either. Our naked hearts were safe with each other.

By the time we got married after three and a half years, we already felt married—in a good way. In fact, we had gone back and forth on whether to legalize our status, for fear that we'd screw it up.

"Why get married? As it is now, we choose to be together and not because we're legally bound. We aren't going to have more children and we've decided to keep our finances separate for the most part," I said.

"True," Matt agreed, adding, "Besides, if we get married, we could jinx it and start taking each other for granted."

I concurred, gun-shy about the possibility of another divorce. After a couple of years of indecision, though, we found a reason that made sense: we would make a binding commitment to our girls that we were a solid, day-in-and-day-out family. Our five daughters had witnessed families falling apart. We would sing it from the California treetops that they could bank on this one.

In 1999 or 2000 we saw Mary Zimmerman's refashioned version of Ovid's *Metamorphoses* at the Berkeley Repertory Theatre. The stage was an immense pool of water with a network of wooden boardwalks for the actors to cross and recross. An aged couple was walking through the magical waterscape, bent over, holding hands and leaning on one another. They died together, holding hands, and a tree grew where they had stood entwined. After the show was over, I stayed in my seat, sobbing uncontrollably, knowing that Matt and I would not share this finale. Once home, we talked about ourselves as seamless parts of one being. For the first time he told me he was uneasy whenever I traveled on my increasingly frequent business trips. "Every time you go away, I worry something will happen. You talk as if you know you will lose me, as if you'll live forever. You don't know that. I'd be devastated if anything happened to you. You have no idea."

On September 18, 2001, when we were still in deep mourning a week after the attacks on the World Trade Center, Matt was diagnosed with stage four esophageal cancer. He hadn't been feeling well and had gone through a number of tests at the hospital, but we didn't expect the chilling diagnosis of zero chance of survival, with six to eighteen months to live. He was sixty-nine and I was fifty-seven.

I took care of him, working at home three days a week and going to the office on the two days my four stepdaughters took half-day turns covering for me. To maintain my sanity, I stayed busy with concrete tasks: helping him dress and shower; positioning and repositioning pillows behind his back (the cancer had invaded his spine and several organs); administering morphine, hydromorphone, and other pain killers prescribed by the oncologist; taking him for acupuncture, chemo, and radiation treatments; driving him to a clinic for the Asian herbal treatments recommended by both his primary care physician and oncologist; feeding him fiber- and protein-enriched smoothies as his appetite waned; finding soothing music to calm him when he got agitated; and Googling during the midnight hours to see if I could find a magic-bullet clinical trial to move the zero survival outlook up a notch. But there was nothing. I tried to hide my despair, but Matt knew. He said, "Sarah, if love were the cure, I'd live forever."

Matt and I had always been physically and verbally animated—we'd coexisted in swirls of hyper motion and dizzying conversation. But post-diagnosis he sat quietly, uncomplaining for the most part; he dozed fitfully in an overstuffed leather recliner in the back den, hoping for a pain-free half an hour now and then. Sometimes he read and listened to his music, but it was hard for him to settle down. I could tell when he was agitated from the way he twitched his feet, the signal that he was feeling out of sorts. I would bend down to his knee level to talk with him softly and slowly, and ask if I could do something to make him more comfortable. One day he said, "Sarah, thank you for slowing down. I know it's hard for you. I get rattled when too much is going on." I kissed him and held back the tears that were always behind my eyes, "Matt, sweetheart, I will do anything to make you feel less rattled. Anything. Just tell me."

"Sallie," he said, using my given name, which he rarely did, "this is our finest hour."

As much as he loved his inner circle of vocalists—Frank Sinatra, Louis Armstrong, Tony Bennett, Ella Fitzgerald, and their musical colleagues—he stopped listening to them. Vocals jangled his nerves, and he could only tolerate instrumental music, preferably the 1930s and 1940s tunes his much older sisters had introduced him to as a preteen as they taught their baby brother to waltz and foxtrot in the kitchen. One morning, I was in a coffee shop a block from our house, getting a latte. Piano music was playing in the background. I recognized "Sentimental Journey," "Body and Soul," and "Seems Like Old Times." That music was the best medicine I could imagine for Matt. I asked the owner if she was selling CDs of the music she was playing.

It wasn't a CD. It was a cassette of music that a young friend of hers played on the piano at the shop from time to time. I asked when the pianist was likely to return. She told me, "It's not a regular thing—Jason drops in when he can, between jobs. Sometimes he helps me do the dishes. I can give you his phone number."

Within minutes I was home, calling Jason Myers to see if I could buy the cassette I'd just heard. He said, "Sure. I'm putting out my CD in March and will call you when it's ready." I told him of Matt's situation, emphasizing the critical timing. "It's for my husband. He's dying, and March will be too late."

Jason said he'd leave a tape at the coffee shop the following day, but wouldn't accept payment. "If your husband likes, I'll come over to your house. I can bring my keyboard and play for him," he said.

"Thank you. That's so kind of you. I doubt that he will accept, but I'll ask him." Matt had been avoiding our friends and would allow only his daughters and two men friends to visit. Not wanting to be an object of pity, he talked briefly with others on the phone, but not in person.

Matt was delighted with the tape and wanted to hear more of this young man's piano playing. He stunned me by accepting the offer of a private concert. I invited Matt's two older daughters, Melanie and Beth, to make it a festive afternoon. Later the girls told me they'd been apprehensive—what they actually said is, "We thought you were crazy"—but I'd been insistent. I thought it would seem less like a funeral with them there. We could attempt to keep it lighthearted. Upbeat emotionally as well as musically.

The gathering was an overwhelming success. For the first time Matt left the recliner and settled into a less comfortable chair in the living room, propped up with pillows. Jason played for an hour and a half, charming us all. Except for Matt, we drank wine and ate cheese and crackers. Matt and Jason conversed animatedly between songs, matching wits as they shared a range of musical anecdotes.

Matt, roused from weeks of semi-lethargy, told Jason our cat had been named in honor of his favorite composer, Hoagy Carmichael. "Did you know Hoagy's father insisted he go to law school because he was sure no one could make a living writing melodies and performing in clubs?" Matt asked. Jason nodded.

"And did you know his parents named him Hoagland after a family of circus performers, the Hoaglands, who had stayed at the Carmichaels' home while Mrs. Carmichael was pregnant?" Jason hadn't known the origin of the name Hoagland, but did know Hoagy's mother had taught him to sing and play the piano at an early age, just as Jason's grandmother had taught him.

From that point on, they parried like old friends drinking beer at a favorite neighborhood bar, discussing Tin Pan Alley songwriters Harold Arlen and Irving Berlin, as well as Johnny Mercer, the Gershwins, and Louis Armstrong, with Jason and Matt tit-for-tatting one another with snippets of music trivia. The daughters and I were speechless at Matt's energy. And at Jason's ability to match and even better Matt, a serious music historian, at least half the time. For one magical afternoon the old Matt was back.

Matt remained seated as Jason prepared to leave; they shook hands as the rest of us stood and hugged. "Thank you for a beautiful time," I said, and we all hugged again.

"I'd like to come play for you again after the holidays," Jason volunteered. Matt accepted with a thumbs-up sign.

December crawled by. The house was a twenty-four-hour sickroom, with Matt's daughters and me doing everything possible to keep him pain free. Hospice services had been authorized, and I wanted them to help out, but even toward the end Matt wouldn't hear of it. He knew hospice meant there was no chance he'd make it, since they required patients to stop all treatment except palliative care. Once he went into a coma, however, I called them. Among their countless helpful acts and words of counsel was the advice that I be prepared for Matt to die when I was not at his side. One volunteer told me, "We don't know why, but patients often die right after their loved ones have left the room. Maybe they don't want to disappoint their loved ones by giving up. Maybe it's to spare them the pain of watching them die. Maybe it's because they want to die alone. Whatever the reason, it happens all the time—they can't choose to keep living indefinitely, but they can choose the moment to go."

On the third day of his coma, his youngest daughter, Claire, spent the night. After a few sleepless hours lying in a sleeping bag on the floor next to his hospital bed, I got up at five to take a shower. I leaned over his bed and told him, "Matt, sweetie, I'm taking a quick shower. I'll be back in less than ten minutes." He gave no indication he'd heard. I touched his hand, kissed him on the cheek, and went into the living room, where Claire was asleep on the sofa bed. I woke her and asked her to stay with her father while I was in the bathroom. Halfway through my shower, she knocked, opening the door before I had a chance to respond. "Sallie, Dad's gone. He's gone." All I remember is being stunned. Despite the conversation with the hospice worker, I couldn't accept that Matt had opted to give up his fight while I was away.

I wasn't with him.

As it turned out, neither was Claire. Later she told me, "That morning, just after you went to the shower, I was looking out the living room window at the early morning sunlight. I think I was just taking a moment to get mentally ready for another hard day. Then I felt as if something brushed my shoulder and I sat up, startled and thought, *Daddy has a beautiful sunrise for leaving*, and I got all teared up. I felt almost sure he'd passed, almost as if he went right out the front door. I went into the back room, and he was gone. And I know this must sound New Agey and weird, but I have always believed that he somehow brushed my shoulder as he left. I know you wanted to be there with him, but how like him to protect you until the end, protect both of us, really, and slip out when you were busy and I hadn't gone in to be with him yet."

We called Claire's sisters, and I notified hospice. A volunteer came to the house to oversee the process from our end, while an off-site volunteer contacted the ambulance company, the cremation society, and the county coroner. Spared the burden of managing the administrative details of his death, the girls and I busied ourselves with dressing Matt. We wanted to remember him in his signature garb, variations of which he wore seven days a week, even to work—blue jeans, a long-sleeved checked shirt, a much-loved leather vest, and his sartorial trademark, a hat. We even managed to share a familial laugh while reviewing his ample hat collection, choosing one that was sun- and sweat-worn from years of family bike rides. At the last minute daughter Sally ran out to the back deck to retrieve a flat, black polished stone from one of Matt's many bonsai plants and put it in his vest pocket. He often carried a stone in his pocket and would take it out, enthusiastically educating us about its sheen, the smoothness, the black glow. Then we watched as the ambulance driver and his assistant placed his stone-graced body on a gurney, covered him with a blanket, and rolled him out the door, down the front walkway, and away from us. Away from our home, our life together. Away from me.

It was January 4, 2002, three and a half months after his diagnosis, twenty-four years after our ice cream store meeting, and two weeks shy of our twentieth wedding anniversary.

10

"JUST BREATHE"

(Both Pearl Jam and Willie Nelson versions)

In mid-January I phoned Jason and, before I said anything other than, "Hi, this is Sallie," he said, "Would you like me to come back and play for you?" I stammered for a moment and replied, "Yes, but at the Berkeley Unitarian Church at the end of the month. Matt died a couple days after New Year's."

The service was held in the high-ceilinged glass atrium of the church on a crystal clear day. From the East Bay Hills we had a panoramic view of San Francisco Bay and the city. Six of Matt's boyhood friends from his Brooklyn days came, as did his two nephews, sons of his two sisters. Friends of Matt's from work and his men's group, as well as couples with whom we'd socialized for more than two decades, attended. Many of my friends and work colleagues came, several flying in from Los Angeles and the East Coast. With wine flowing and a cornucopia of hors d'oeuvres, it could have been a cocktail party. Jason, in a snazzy pin-striped suit, enthusiastically played Fats Waller before and after the service. It was the rare woman there who didn't fall for the coolest, dearest piano player they'd ever seen or heard, a man who has become my substitute son.

In three and a half months, Matt had gone from using a cane, to a walker, then a wheelchair, and ultimately a hospital bed. I believed I was fully prepared for the inevitable. A diagnosis of zero percent chance of survival leaves no room for optimism. I harbored no illusions, but was still gobsmacked by the unexpected quiet and emptiness in the house. How could it be that there was nothing left to show that he'd filled up the place so completely? I was hung up on my high school understanding of Einstein's $E=mc^2$. Matter didn't go away, it converted itself into energy. Where had that take-over-the-house energy gone?

Matt had been my foundation, the floor I counted on and joyously skipped and danced on for a quarter of a century. Without him I foresaw endless years ahead of tripping and stumbling with nothing underneath me. Unable to absorb the finality of a Matt-less existence, I immersed myself in books about overcoming grief, most importantly Pema Chodron's *When Things Fall Apart* and Rabbi Harold Kushner's *When Bad Things Happen to Good People*. I read selected passages over and over, occasionally reaching brief moments of peace and acceptance. Much of what both the Buddhist nun and the Jewish rabbi wrote moved me, but especially relevant was Pema Chodron's chapter on hopelessness. I felt one hundred percent hopeless, convinced that my pain and loneliness would never lessen. Chodron's metaphor of the ground paralleled mine of a foundation; she wrote of the unstable ground that won't stop rocking as we attempt to remain standing. Chodron was unequivocal that there is no comforting hand. I tried to absorb the truth of her declaration. Matt was gone and, with that finality, gone were the consoling hands and arms, the words of comfort, the soul mate at my side. She stressed that reaching a state of hopelessness about having someone or something to hold on to is the beginning of the journey toward cheerfulness, wisdom, and clarity. I understood the state of hopelessness—it was the part about becoming cheerful and wise that gave me trouble.

We all lose people. Some move on as we age or relocate or our circumstances change. Some betray us. And some die, and those left behind, Chodron says, feel like a pile of shit. I found it refreshing that this spiritually rich woman not only did not hesitate to swear, she went further. The path to healing, she clarified, called for fully examining the properties of the shit. Touching it. Smelling it. If I could do that, I told myself, maybe then I could accept it and move on. And I got it, over and over I got it, for maybe fifteen minutes at a time; then I'd lose it, and the pain and yearning for Matt resurged. I wanted his hand, his chest, his voice, his mind. I wanted my floor. I felt hopeless about embracing hopelessness.

I latched on to another piece of writing, Lydia Davis' brilliant poem "Head Heart," and slipped a photocopy of its few lines into my copy of *When Things Fall Apart.*

> *Heart is so new to this.*
> *I want them back, says heart.*
> *Head is all heart has.*
> *Help, head. Help heart.*

As an agnostic, I asked my brain to do what the poet asks of her brain: help my disbelieving heart to accept that Matt was gone.

My head told me to keep busy. Working out at a gym three days a week and walking four miles a day were good ways to burn up my frenetic energy but didn't help me sleep at night. I lost twenty-five pounds and became scrawny. For a year I continued working in San Francisco, going through the motions at a job I had previously loved. My coworkers and my boss, the bank president and a dear friend to this day, were patient and supportive. Between grief counseling sessions, I volunteered at an animal shelter.

And then there was Clyde. Shortly after Matt died, I ran across a posting on PAWS (Pets Are Wonderful Support), a San Francisco-based organization that trains and provides service dogs to individuals with disabilities. A two-year-old golden retriever service dog in Berkeley needed exercise and play time. Clyde's job supporting Dave, a quadriplegic college student, was demanding. Dave's morning and evening aides gave Clyde two daily ten-minute trips outdoors to pee and poo. The rest of the time he was at Dave's side, keeping him company in the apartment, picking up things Dave dropped, and putting them on his lap. When Dave went to class, doctors' appointments, and physical and occupational therapy sessions, Clyde was tethered to Dave's battery-operated wheelchair. The magnificent animal guided Dave across busy Berkeley streets and, once inside the classroom or office, settled noiselessly at Dave's feet for hours, waiting for a pencil to drop, so he could return it. On more than a few occasions Dave's wheelchair ran over Clyde's tail, and Clyde, trained to tolerate pain, barely whimpered.

Clyde became part of my ongoing routine, a job I shared with another couple who loved Clyde as much as I did. Once or twice a week until he retired nine years later, I took Clyde out for hour-long romps in the park. I removed his blue-and-yellow service dog cape, and the golden boy got to be a carefree puppy, chasing a ball, running like the wind, and getting pats and rubs from admiring passers-by. To encourage people to pet him, I would tell them he was a service dog whose owner was physically unable to touch him, and that Clyde spent every waking hour on wheelchair duty. "He can't get petted when he's wearing his cape, which is almost always. Pet him some more," I urged them, pointing to the silky-haired creature lying on his back, giddily moving four legs in the air and joyously wagging his tail. And they would keep petting. The only thing Clyde wasn't allowed to do was play with other dogs, regardless of how much he whined to engage with his fellow canines. The rules were strict: it was important that interactions with other dogs be limited, or he might lose some of his working-dog orientation.

As much as I loved Clyde, I wanted my own dog. We'd had to give up our hyperactive German shorthaired pointer when Matt became sick. We found her the perfect home, with a stay-at-home adult, a huge yard, and a pool to swim in. I found a calmer replacement who adjusted easily to my small living space and didn't need four hours of exercise a day: Clementine, a large-headed, small-bodied, stubby-legged rescue dog, a mix of German shepherd (the head) and longhaired dachshund (the rest). Named after Winston Churchill's loving and long-suffering wife, Clemmie joined my two indoor house cats with nary a hiss or a bark from either side. Her soulful brown eyes and enthusiastic wiggles provided me with free around-the-clock therapeutic support. I rescued my "spare-parts dog," as a girlfriend called her, and then she rescued me.

The life I crafted was both similar to and very different from the old one. I went to the same movie theaters and restaurants, sometimes with friends, but more often alone. I continued taking adult education courses. Weekdays were tolerable, partly because my married girlfriends were available to do things without their husbands and partly because I made sure to keep a hectic schedule. But I dreaded the nights and weekends, especially weekend nights. I often went from Friday afternoon till Monday morning without seeing a friend. Saturday and Sunday nights were endless. I checked my watch continually to see how many hours remained till Monday, when I could meet a friend at the gym or for lunch. I turned visits to a coffee shop and the cleaners into social events and chatted longer than a cappuccino or stained pair of pants warranted. I approached dog-walking locals on the street, eager for stories of strays that had been found at a shelter and were now loved beyond measure. In time I got back to scratching in the dirt and pruning our roses, but it took a while. Matt and I had gardened together, and solo gardening was a bleak activity.

After Matt died, I added two quotes to the collection of notes and recipes, cartoons and photos of beloved pets on my refrigerator. They have guided me, sometimes successfully and sometimes not, through my dark-night-of-the-soul periods.

The first reads: "Never never never give up—Winston Churchill." However, what the British Prime Minister actually said is, "Never give in, never, never, never, never—in nothing, great or small, large or petty—never give in, except to convictions of honour and good sense." He delivered this message in desperate times, when Great Britain was alone in fighting Hitler in Europe, after Poland, France, Czechoslovakia, and the Low Countries were defeated and before Roosevelt committed America to the war effort.

To Matt and me, Churchill was a hero without equal. Twice we visited the Churchill War Rooms in London, and we went to Chartwell, his private home in Southeast England. Winston Churchill's example has sustained me twice through black-hole times—after I divorced Daniel and floundered with a small child and barely tolerable jobs in San Francisco and again, twenty-eight years later, when Matt died. If Churchill could guide an entire country through disastrous times while everything caved around him throughout Europe, couldn't I recover from the loss of one person? I would go on living for Heather and my parents, but could honestly think of no other reasons.

The second quote addresses personal tragedy on a life- and body-crushing scale. The actor Christopher Reeve's fall from a horse in 1995 destroyed his first and second cervical vertebrae; the connection between his skull and spine was severed. He spent the rest of his life in a wheelchair, breathing with a portable ventilator, unable to move below the neck. Even so, the actor we know from the movies as Superman stood tall. I read somewhere that he'd said after his accident, "People don't fail. They just stop trying." This quote has been attributed to others, but whether or not he originated these words, they could have been his creed. How could I, able-bodied, healthy, and financially secure, stop trying? He hadn't.

My coping mechanisms to fill the emptiness at home still included work, gym classes, endless walking, volunteer work, and time with girlfriends, but they weren't doing the trick. I was failing in a number of basic life activities. I kept forgetting to turn off the stove and close the front door when I left the house; I transposed phone numbers routinely. I ran stop signs and had three car accidents that were my fault—I didn't see cars that were right in front of me.

Over the next year I continued working, using my accumulated vacation every several months to go to New Orleans, in rotation with my sister, to help our overburdened eighty-eight-year-old mother care for our ninety-three-year-old father, afflicted with dementia, diabetes, flesh-eating bacteria, and numerous stroke-related impairments.

As much as I loved my mother, I never cottoned to her lifelong aspiration that I become a socially prominent New Orleanian. I failed her when I left Daniel, even though he was "a good man," as she commented numerous times—which he definitely was. Later, when I confided in her that Bob drank excessively, she seemed to forget she had told me that drinking was one of the few justifications to leave a marriage—after all, he would be a good father for Heather. Besides, he was part of the upper echelons of San Francisco.

And then, adding insult to injury, I failed her once again by falling head over heels for a Brooklyn-born Jew with an ex-wife and four daughters to support. His parents hadn't even gone to high school. He would never be able to support me in style. I told her I didn't care a whit (I might have used the unacceptable word "shit") about her objections on cultural, religious, ethnic, and financial grounds. I could support myself and Heather. Besides, I considered his four daughters a plus in our lives, not a minus. For a while, she and I barely communicated, and I stopped going to New Orleans.

Over time, Mom saw how interconnected Matt and I were. She came to appreciate how impressive his daughters were and how they reached out to Heather. My parents began visiting us in Berkeley (but only after we were married). Without even trying, Matt won my mother over. She respected his wide range of knowledge about American and European history, especially World Wars I and II. She was fascinated by his interest in making wine and cultivating bonsai trees. She shared his love of 1940s music, the music she and Dad had danced to at the various officers' clubs.

But Matt never forgot Mom's objections to his being Jewish and her earlier rebukes for our premarital shacking up. I forgave much more easily than he did. I understood the public humiliation she had experienced living with a ne'er-do-well father who'd been openly womanizing, drinking, and gambling. For years my grandmother had kept the family going, with the help of two industrious sons and Mom, who, at thirteen, worked as a caretaker for an elderly neighbor every day after school. I knew she wanted the best for me, but she mistakenly thought what was best for her was best for me. Over the years, as her objections to Matt disappeared, we grew as close as we'd been when I was a child.

And I'd never forgotten the good times. My mother had a great sense of humor. Every summer she gave a buffet luncheon for at least a hundred ladies, and she always dressed up. One year she wore my sister's pink chiffon high school prom dress, although she couldn't zip it up after gaining weight over the years. So she cut out the back of the dress and wore a strapless corset and polka-dot bloomers on her otherwise unclothed back side. She put Spanish moss on her head. As she opened the door for her proper uptown pals to enter, she introduced herself as the Blimpy Nymph from Nymphenburg.

After Matt died and I quit work, I spent weeks at a time in New Orleans, helping out with Dad. I could see she was frazzled, but she inevitably maintained, "He wants me and no one else. I can do this." She always said, "Besides, when I know you're coming to help me, my load lightens just knowing you'll be here soon. And after you leave, I still feel the glow from your visit. Sal, you're my maypole."

In fall of the following year, my father died after nine years of an increasingly diminished life. His long ordeal was over. I had loved him, but the dad I knew had been gone for years. He had been a demanding but loving parent, one who expected obedience but was predictable and steady. Being a peacemaker and "the good child," I knew his limits and had observed them. (Virginia, on the other hand, was more rebellious than I was, and they got into occasional scrapes.) He had taught me to throw a softball; we'd spent many hours outside playing catch, and he was proud I didn't "throw like a sissy washerwoman," whatever that meant.

My mother said his military career had brought out traits she hadn't seen in the sweet small-town Alabama boy she met on a blind date to a Tulane football game. Dad told me he knew on their first date she was "the one." Mom told me over and over, "I married him because he tasted good. And I knew I could trust him." They were married for sixty-seven devoted years.

My mother Virginia, named after her mother, just as my sister was named after Mom, had been at his side during his decline, turning our home into a hospital room. The dining room table was relocated to our foyer to hold medications, creams, gauze, and diapers. His hospital bed occupied the space where for forty years scores of guests had laughed, eaten, and sipped, their wine glasses shimmering under the chandelier. Behind the headboard, Mom had installed a pulley to help raise him up, so his lungs wouldn't be congested. Dad was in and out of the hospital several times toward the end, and our mother spent entire days and most nights sitting up in a chair, watching over him.

This eighty-eight-year-old dynamo had exhausted herself. Gin and I begged her to get caretakers to help her or put him in a care facility, but she wouldn't. "He's my husband, and I love him. You wouldn't have done that with Matt," she told me. That was true, but Matt only lived a few months after his diagnosis. And I was fifty-seven, not pushing ninety. When my father died, Virginia and I were relieved that Mom could finally get some much-needed rest. It was past time for our maternal Wonder

Woman to kick up her Auntie Mame heels at luncheons, bridge parties, and outings with her many friends.

But Mom was not well. Having refused to leave my father's side during his hospital stays, she had caught *Clostridium difficile*, or *C. diff*, resulting in severe diarrhea and colitis. She landed in the same hospital where Dad had been. Gin and I raced from California and Washington, DC, to help her recuperate, and our invincible mother bounced back. We were sure she was getting better when she was able to do the three things she had said she wanted to do after Dad died: play bridge and win, wear her new black-and-red dress, and give a book review to a ladies' group. She did all three, the last to thundering applause.

For the last several years of my father's life, we'd been promising Mom that, when he was gone, we'd take her back to Fürstenfeldbruck, outside of Munich, and help her find as many of "her girls" as we could. At age thirty-one, with two daughters aged five and three years old, Mother had joined her husband for his three-year assignment in post-World War II Germany. She was appalled to find the conditions in which the German children were growing up. The US Army was mounting a de-Nazification campaign for the boys who'd been part of the Hitler Youth movement. Service men sponsored baseball, football, and basketball teams, English classes, movie outings, and camping weekends. Mom, planning a similar program for girls from ages five to eighteen, went to the base commander and asked for a site—an abandoned restaurant—and a monthly allotment of coal. She received both. With the help of other officers' wives, Mom organized activities: swimming, diving, cooking, debate, reading, gymnastics, English, and, on Fridays, Bingo. She made sure to have snacks every afternoon, since many of these girls ate only one meal a day. She even commissioned a pilot friend to bring back oranges and, if possible, bananas from North Africa. One child had never seen an orange and thought it was a ball. One mother, seeing a banana for the first time in four years, wept.

Running Bingo on Friday afternoons was the high point of Mom's week. She hit up her friends on the base, especially those about to be transferred back to the US, for Bingo prizes. The winners received a dish here, a sweater there, or a doll or teddy bear. Even bars of soap were treasures. When we left Fürstenfeldbruck in 1949, 219 girls showed up at the train station to present our mother with a bouquet of red roses. They threw roses at our compartment window as our family started our trip back to the States.

But Gin and I were not able to keep our promise to reunite her with her girls. Mom contracted *C. diff* a second time and was prescribed an excessively strong dosage of Cipro that triggered a heart attack. She died on a Saturday morning in late November, less than two and a half months after my father. Thankfully our lovely next-door neighbor, Barbara Adler, was with Mom. Since Gin and I had left, Barbara had been stopping by regularly to see how our mother was doing. She removed Mom's nightgown to perform CPR. Barbara phoned me immediately. "She didn't suffer long. When the ambulance came, she was gone. And I know this sounds strange for me to say, but your mother had a beautiful bosom. As if she were far younger than her years."

Mom was young. To this day, I think of her when I hear Rod Stewart's "Forever Young." She is forever young in my sister's heart and in mine.

Heather and me: the single-mom days.

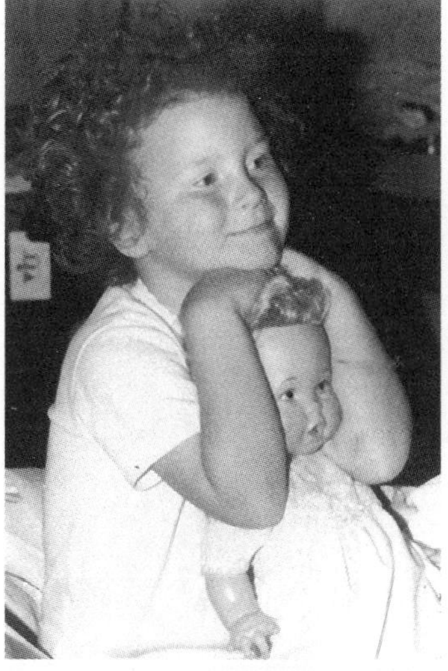

A favorite picture
of Heather.

My Apache pilot daughter,
serving in Kosovo
(and she never learned to
drive a standard shift car).

Matt's photo, sent in response to my personals ad. If it hadn't been for a postal rate increase, we wouldn't have met.

Stepping out to go dancing in San Francisco: an attempt to imitate Fred and Ginger.

Matt's jerry-rigged photo of us in Lourdes, France.

Pianist Jason Myers playing for my stepdaughter Claire's wedding (mid 2000s).

My parents, Steve and Virginia, in front of their home in New Orleans.

Clyde, the wondrous service dog.

Team PASTRAMI compatriots, sister Virginia and her son Clayton. The monkey was our mascot, reminding us to keep monkey business and humor thriving during my search.

Project PASTRAMI...

A Site about Love (and Monkey Business)

- Be a PASTRAMI Love Liaison - help your friend, friend of a friend, relative, or colleague become a PASTRAMI Candidate and look forward to his Saturday nights (and all days and nights) again. Help Sallie discover a life partner within the PASTRAMI parameters.
- Be a PASTRAMI Candidate! Bring your PASTRAMI ingredients to the rich mix.
- Go to the website to find out what Project PASTRAMI is

  ...(and it's not about a meat sandwich).

WIN $5,000 FOR YOUR FAVORITE NON-PROFIT ORGANIZATION

Website: projectpastrami.squarespace.com

Email: projectpastrami@gmail.com

Every day in the Dominican
Republic, we set up a clinic
in an area like this . . .

. . . where I found a tiny bit
of Grace (who's since taken
on the name Tillie Grace).

Backyard in Berkeley,
with canines McGee and
Tillie Grace.

Trekking in the mountains
of the Sacred Valley in Peru,
knowing I'd never reach the peak—
and knowing it didn't matter.

The Haiken family outings are a longstanding
fall tradition. Here we are in Mendocino in 2019.

Hiking with Marcia, Bart, and
Bart's Sulay (aka "White Fang") along the
Metolius River in Central Oregon.

Dinner with Bart at
one of our favorite
restaurants, this one on the
southern Oregon coast.

Marcia, our
matchmaker, insisted on
being our flower girl.

Our wedding day: Louisiana lady in red with her Mississippi man.

Thank you, Universe.

11

"IL SILENZIO"

(Melissa Venema version)

The black hole in my heart doubled in size.

Having settled Matt's estate the previous year, I was an executor once again. I focused my manic energy on selling my parents' home and disposing of their belongings. With my share of the proceeds, I bought a small shotgun-style house in New Orleans, eight blocks from the family home. I spent time with remaining family members and longtime friends, taking security-blanket pooch Clemmie with me. Then in late August 2005, Hurricane Katrina decimated the city. The levees gave way, flooding "The City that Care Forgot" and "The Big Easy." The rescue and recovery effort proved to be a national embarrassment, given FEMA's anemic emergency response to the area's dire need for electricity, clean water, sanitation, food, shelter, and medical care. Blue tarps covered the damaged roofs of a majority of houses a year or more after the water subsided.

Thousands of duct-taped refrigerators lined the sidewalks; abandoned cars remained on the raised grassy areas in the middle of major streets. Garbage collection was suspended indefinitely. The chaos continued for months and in some neighborhoods for years. Compared to the eighty percent of the city submerged in rancid water for weeks during record heat, I got off lightly. My fixer-upper house, still under renovation, lost part of the roof and all of a fence, but suffered no interior water damage. It took two months before I could get a flight to New Orleans and many more before I could replace my refrigerator, find workers to repair my house, and buy milk at a local grocery store.

I went to Germany to spend Christmas with my daughter Heather, now thirty-five. After the previous year, a change of scenery and some holiday festivities would be welcome.

My first and only child was an easy baby, happy, healthy, energetic, and alert. She began walking at ten months and by age four was reading. The bubbly Campbell soup kid turned into a stunning Raggedy Ann with barely tamed curly red strands around her face. But at the same time Heather's body was stretching out into the fashion model she could have been, she began turning inward, uncomfortable with people commenting on her hair and with being singled out for her intelligence. When people on the street smiled and called her "Red," she invariably demanded I tell them to stop. She didn't believe it was a compliment. At school she made few friendships with children her age; she was more comfortable with her teachers and with my friends than with her age-appropriate peers. In second grade, when her Montessori teachers suggested she skip a grade, I said no. My parents and I thought Heather would do better not being singled out for her smarts; we worried that being thrown in with older kids might highlight her lack of social skills. To offset this imbalance, as she moved through grade school, she participated in activities where she thrived—ice skating, swimming, doll house crafts, and a Saturday sports program. On weekends she and I went bicycle riding and enjoyed an array of art projects together. Once or twice a year, when I could afford it, we went skiing at Lake Tahoe.

But after Heather started seventh grade, she joined a peer group awash in alcohol and drugs. It took a year for me to understand that she wasn't merely a snarly, bratty adolescent moving through a normal developmental stage toward independence from her mother. One evening I found her passed out in the bushes in the front yard. I called an ambulance to take her to the hospital and stayed with her while the doctors pumped her stomach. I held the child I had once been able to protect but no longer could. She started a drug rehab program, and we attended extended family therapy sessions. The therapist, believing Heather was going through a phase, felt certain she would move through it.

The so-called phase lasted throughout high school. Though she was a National Merit semifinalist, Heather barely graduated because she skipped so much school. I had no idea she wasn't showing up for exams and was failing some courses. She made A's in classes she liked, with teachers she respected, and C's, D's, and F's in others. Her SAT scores and College Board results enabled her to get into San Diego State, but she still skipped class and dipped into this and that drug. During Christmas of her sophomore year, unbeknownst to me, Heather dropped out of college. I was frantic. For three months I didn't know if she was alive. Eventually, I found out she had joined the Army, which turned her life around. She told me that the Army conducted unannounced intermittent drug testing on its soldiers, and, to my relief, she admitted it would keep her "on the straight and narrow."

Steeped in the ethic of her two career military officer grandfathers, Heather finished her college degree, graduated with honors, and began working on her master's in business administration, with an emphasis in airport management. She went to flight school at Fort Rucker, Alabama, again graduating with honors. For some years she flew an Apache helicopter, serving in Kosovo.

One evening she called me on the phone and proudly said, "Mom, today I flew over Sniper Alley in Sarajevo." I was stunned, proud, and terrified that my daughter, who'd never learned to drive a stick-shift car, had flown twenty-five feet above an area where a sniper could end her life in a second. When I asked her if she'd been frightened, she answered with only a trace of the old edge to her voice, "Mom, I'm a soldier. This is what I do."

Indeed it was. Heather excelled in winter survival skills as she proved when she and five male soldiers went on a grueling exercise, following the Army's strict protocols in the forests of Norway. She was the only one to succeed in every category: she scavenged for food, built a fire, found cover to avoid freezing to death, and made her way back to civilization with her compass and minimal supplies. All the men were deemed to have failed on one count or another and to have "died" by operational criteria.

On another occasion she was staying in a bivouac shelter for several days with a large group of soldiers, both male and female. Her cot was placed in a section near a few of the men. When she went to the bathroom, two of the men decided to pull a prank on her. They put a rubber snake in her cot, covering it with the top sheet and her blanket. When she returned and pulled back the covers, a realistic-looking snake was coiled in anticipation. Without hesitation, and without a sound, she grabbed her .45 pistol and shot it. They shouldn't have been surprised by the quick action of my sharpshooter daughter.

Heather's plan was to put in twenty years with the Army as a pilot, retire at thirty-nine, and ultimately work in civilian airport operations. But after sustaining multiple spinal disc injuries from parachuting, she had been grounded, much to her dismay, and assigned to administrative jobs, first in Brussels and then in Heidelberg with SHAPE (Supreme Headquarters Allied Powers Europe). I visited her in both places, amazed and gratified that the willful, bitchy teenager had turned into a confident, hardworking model of self-discipline. We spoke every weekend, emailed, and got together regularly when she was stationed in the States and less frequently when she was overseas.

The road from turbulent teenager to loving, drug-free adult daughter had brought us to a good place. In December 2005, we had ten special days together, traveling in castle- and forest-rich Germany, beading earrings and necklaces, watching DVDs, and playing with her cats. We went to Christmas markets, walked in the snow, and sipped hot chocolate with whipped cream in cafés as German carols were piped in through the sound system. We cooked her favorite recipes and stuffed her freezer with enough New Orleans jambalaya and spinach Madeleine for her to invite friends to dinner for weekends to come. Just after Christmas, she drove me back to the Frankfurt airport. As always when we parted, we had the next vacation planned. In six months, I would be back and we would explore more of Germany or tour the Dordogne in France. We kissed each other good-bye.

On the morning of January 4, 2006, the fourth anniversary of Matt's death, I sat at my computer, weeping quietly as I began typing my journal entry: "I should be further along by now. Back to normal, getting on with it, happier about things. I'm not getting there, wherever 'there' is. I am a flat stick figure, always in meaningless motion. If I stop and force myself to stay still, the pain becomes unbearable." I was straining to find the words to convey my sentiments and impatient and disappointed in myself for needing to pour it all out. "Why can't I get over this? Why am I stuck after four years? I have to move on with my life." The words of Churchill and Reeve weren't getting through my head to my heart.

Clementine was doing what she did whenever I was sad. My high-EQ mutt had trotted on her stubby legs across the four rooms separating us and was staring at me, her head resting on my left knee. Her unblinking brown eyes, fixed on my face, seemed to say, "I'm here. We're together."

When the doorbell rang, I ignored it, willing the Mormons or Jehovah's Witnesses who frequented our neighborhood to move on. I kept typing; the doorbell kept ringing. I got up angrily, prepared to order the unwelcome visitors to keep their comments about heaven and salvation to themselves. But instead there was a middle-aged, dark-haired woman in an Army uniform with the insignia of a full colonel, my dad's insignia. She had a kindly, but uncomfortable, look on her face. Introducing herself as Col. Something, she asked gently, "May I come in?" Without thinking, I said in a sharp tone, "Not unless you tell me Heather's okay." She repeated her request, "May I come in?" I rephrased my response, "Is Heather okay?" A third time she asked, "May I come in and talk with you?" At this point I raised my voice—I was most likely yelling, "Tell me, goddammit, is Heather dead?" She said, "Yes, she is. May I come in?" I remember hearing myself say, "Come in," and thinking, *This cannot be happening.*

Not happening. Not today. Not Heather. Not. Can't. Cannotfuckingbehappening. The vibrant five-foot eight-inch redhead in camouflage fatigues, who could have been on the cover of a Victoria's Secret catalogue, was dead from the interaction of medications she took for herniated disc pain with the champagne she drank on New Year's Eve. To my knowledge, this was the first time she'd ignored the proscription against drinking alcohol while on pain meds. She'd died in her bed over a three-day holiday weekend while I was leaving short cheery messages on her phone, assuming she was out celebrating with friends. When I arrived at Heather's house in Heidelberg a few days after Col. Something's house call, I played back my three messages, wondering what had been happening at the exact moment I left each greeting. Did she hear any of them? If so, did she think she was dreaming that I was talking to her? If she'd answered the first or even the second call, could she have been saved? *Could I have saved her?*

First there was a service in Heidelberg attended by her friends, and then Heather was buried at Arlington National Cemetery on a beautiful winter day. It was crisp and sunny, with a brisk breeze. My sister and my dear girlfriend Murray were there, as was Heather's father, Daniel, accompanied by his wife, Heather's lovely stepmother. Before the casket was loaded onto the caisson, my sister went into the holding room and, when no one was there, she opened the top of the casket and placed a small packet of my mother's ashes over Heather's heart. I had brought the ashes with me and asked Virginia to do that, but couldn't bring myself to accompany her. I couldn't bear the thought of seeing Heather's red hair.

The caisson with the coffin containing her uniformed body was transported by a team of shiny, dark brown horses to the burial site. It was real and surreal simultaneously. Years later Virginia told me she'd visited Heather's grave several times and asked me if I ever wanted to go visit it, visit her, visit my daughter. "If you decide you want to, I'll go with you." I told Virginia I was pretty sure I wouldn't ever want to go, but was touched that she had gone.

She also recounted an event I had no memory of, "You know, when the honor guard folded the flag into a perfect triangle and handed it to you at Arlington, you refused to take it. You kept your arms at your side. He tried several times to hand it to you, so I took it for you. Then the honor guard gave a flag to Daniel as well." I don't remember that, but was probably thinking, *If I don't accept the flag, it means Heather is still alive.*

I settled a third estate in four years, this time with much-appreciated help from the Army's outstanding casualty support team.

The motto to not give up was more meaningful now than ever, but impossible to absorb. I reread the same dog-eared books and the Lydia Davis poem that had provided solace four years earlier. They didn't help. I increased my exercise regimen and volunteer work, tried to ramp up my meditation practice, and attended a new round of grief counseling sessions. Sleep was elusive, and though I tried to eat, food tasted like sawdust mixed with dirt. My weight plunged once again. I don't remember the conversation, but years later, my sister told me that when she wondered how I'd lost so much weight, I told her, "It's called the death diet." And apparently I added, "I don't recommend it."

I went into individual therapy. I had no life juices left after losing my husband, both parents, and my daughter within four years. My longtime coping strategy, inherited from my father, was to ignore the pain and soldier on. My mother, on the other hand, didn't ignore sadness, but felt it important to put on a good face and cover up. But even she couldn't have covered over the loss of the granddaughter she adored. I am eternally grateful she didn't have to.

I hoped a therapist would help make the grief of losing Heather more bearable, to show me how to integrate it into a place in my heart without being immobilized by it. What I didn't anticipate was that losing my daughter would bring up the other deaths, and, in short order, I found myself reliving the loss of Matt and my parents. As the therapist remarked a number of times over our two and a half years together, "You will never be pain free. Don't expect that. But the pain will lessen from time to time. It already has. That's what I've seen in our sessions so far. The bouts of sadness will continue to diminish in frequency and depth." She also said I would gradually remember more of the good times, more of the joy. That has happened, although I still roll my eyes with annoyance when people say, "Time heals all things." It doesn't. In my opinion, it doesn't even heal most things. But the pain becomes bearable. Barely bearable at times. More so at others.

12

"BRIDGE OVER TROUBLED WATER"

(Simon and Garfunkel version)

For twelve years after Matt's death, I'd spent several weeks each summer doing volunteer work in Latin America, mostly as a medical interpreter. In 2016, however, there was no trip scheduled, so I accepted a friend's invitation to go trekking in the Sacred Valley of Cusco, Peru.

This was my girlfriend Andrea's fourth or fifth trip with Theo, a guide and healer in Cusco. She told me that most days Theo led the group on hikes in the mountains, giving lectures about the history of the indigenous cultures that had lived there and guiding visits to archeological ruins. "I guess you'd call him a shaman," she said, "but he's Western-educated and participates fully in both modern and traditional native cultures." During rest stops and some mornings after breakfast and evenings before dinner, Theo led the group in spiritual work invoking

Pachamama, or Earth Mother, and introducing an assortment of Andean belief systems and traditions.

I knew Andy well from decades of our working together at the Federal Reserve and knew her to be sensible and down-to-earth. If she'd gone on so many trips with Theo, it had to be a valuable experience. I felt a twinge of guilt to be doing something solely for fun and for the joy of being outdoors, but figured I could enjoy not working fourteen-hour days in ninety-degree heat.

We stayed on the outskirts of Cusco, in the suburb of San Jerónimo, at La Casona—"the large house"—built by Theo's grandfather a century earlier in what was then the countryside. Theo, a native of Cusco, PhD cultural anthropologist, former governor of the Cusco region, and accomplished horseback rider and pianist, appeared to be in his early sixties, with the lithe body and carriage of a tennis player. He resembled a distinguished professor, complete with a trimmed salt-and-pepper beard; a narrow, handsome face; and a soft-spoken, authoritative demeanor. He'd converted the family home into an elegant retreat center, with native trees and shrubs, an extensive rose garden, and stone walkways crisscrossing the charming courtyard. Outside on the busy suburban street, buses belched smoke and screeched their brakes, and cars sounded their horns all day long, but inside La Casona's stucco façade peace and quiet reigned in the rustic reception lounge, with overstuffed sofas, tall-backed wooden chairs, and rough-hewn tables.

Most mornings we ate breakfast around seven thirty or eight, then met with Theo for far-ranging and often confusing discussions that touched on an unpredictable jumble of topics, including archeology, history, architecture, indigenous cultures, and abstract spiritual issues. He told us one morning that our goal was to "work toward bridging our conscious and unconscious beings into a single whole." He emphasized that by using native Andean healing techniques, we could reach "a state of gratitude and joy and manage our energy to transform living into an art." I tried to step away from my entrenched linear thinking to figure out what Theo was talking about. That was the only way for me to osmose, however marginally, his messages of openness and wholeness, the embedded consciousness of our ancestors, and a balanced relationship with light, air, water, rocks, mountains, vibrations, and the sun. I was partially successful for brief periods. It wasn't something to think about, so much as something *not* to think about and just accept, clearly a job for heart, not head. Or maybe it was a way of thinking about not thinking.

After our morning sessions, we'd head off for a day of trekking in the Sacred Valley, with snowcapped peaks as a backdrop. We held our breath as the driver maneuvered hairpin turns on the narrow winding roads that took us both lower and much higher than Cusco's eleven-thousand-foot altitude. The names of the places sounded like incantations: Ollantaytambo, Chinchero, Salkantay, Sacsayhuaman, and, of course, Machu Picchu.

Most days we hiked for six or eight hours, gasping for air, swigging water, and tracking the hundreds of feet (or more) of altitude we gained on each outing. We climbed up to fourteenth- and fifteenth-century ruins, where Theo described the spiritual traditions, geology, archeology, and culture of the Incas, as well as the story of the Spaniards' early sixteenth-century invasion that put an end to the Inca Empire.

The highlight of the trip occurred two days before our return to the States. Andy prepared me for what she described as an intense spiritual session with Theo. "You go upstairs after dinner, to a dark, candlelit room. You sit in a circle on the floor for four hours or more, so bring pillows and blankets from your bedroom. Take a jacket because it can get cold. Don't plan on getting out before midnight."

"Why does it go on so long?" I asked.

"Theo talks with each person privately—but 'privately' means he talks to you in a soft voice while others are sitting on the floor nearby." She added, "You don't have to do it if you don't want to. It's voluntary. I've done it a few times and am going to skip this time."

I felt I had nothing to lose and possibly something to gain, as seven of us entered the room and arranged ourselves in a U-shape on the floor, leaning against the wall, with pillows at our backs, blankets on our legs, and bottles of water at our sides. Theo turned off the lights in the room, then returned to his chair, a shadowy figure with a small flashlight to guide his way. He called one person and talked with her for what might have been twenty or twenty-five minutes. Then he called a second person. I lost track of time until Theo called me to approach. I felt unsteady in the dim lighting, concerned that I would trip on someone's outstretched legs. I could barely make out the outline of his body, but could tell where he was from the direction of his voice. He surprised me by addressing me in Spanish, which he hadn't done during our ten days together. But he'd heard me talking with the bus driver, people on the street, and the employees at La Casona. "*¿Por qué andas preocupada? ¿Por qué estás triste?* What worries you? What are you sad about?" he asked.

I hadn't had a single personal conversation with Theo and didn't think I'd projected that image to the group. But he was right. "I'm worried I will never love anyone again, not the way I loved my husband and my daughter. I may never again love at that level, to that depth. I don't love the way I used to, the way I want to."

He asked a few questions, "How did your husband die? When? How did your daughter die? When?" I answered, and he asked, "What have you done to celebrate them? Have they spoken to you?"

I don't recall anything else about our verbal interchange because I was sobbing soundlessly, inside my entire body, so silently that I doubt people sitting in the circle a few feet away from me could hear. I felt the years of sadness flooding through body and soul; I relived the grief of losing the husband and daughter I had loved in a way I desperately wanted to love again. Talking with Theo stripped away the armor I had constructed, which had enabled this colonel's daughter to rise and shine when she wanted to lie down and cry. Theo interspersed his questions with commands for me to move toward him and away from him, turn in different directions, slow down my stride and speed it up, look up and look down, and make motions with my hands. He chanted in a beautiful baritone voice, shook rattles at and around me, rang bells, and waved a large feather up and down my body, front and back, making an eerie whooshing sound.

I stayed with him for about a half hour before he gave me his final instructions and had me repeat them. "*Esto es lo que tienes que hacer.* This is what you must do. You have to do it on the right days and in the right order. You will arrive home on Tuesday. On Friday you start drinking a cup of special tea every morning and washing your face and head in an herbal mixture every morning. You will do this every day until Friday of next week. I will give you the dried herbs for the tea and the wash." I carefully repeated his instructions.

He continued, "Buy three pairs of beeswax candles—one red, one green, and one golden. This Friday night place the red candles by photographs of your husband and your daughter and go to bed with them lit. On Tuesday do the same with the green ones. And next Friday do the same with the golden ones. Let them burn out on their own. Don't blow them out."

When I asked about the meaning of the colors and the importance of the sequence, Theo responded softly, "*Las velas rojas representan la pasión que sientes por ellos. Las verdes son para la regeneración, el renacimiento. Y las doradas iluminarán el camino para ellos y para ti.*" Again I began to sob. "The red candles are for the passion you feel for them. Put a red candle next to each photograph. Think about your passion, your love for them. On Tuesday the green candles will represent spring, regrowth, rebirth. You must think about being reborn. The gold candles will light their way, where they are, their path. And your way, where you are, because you have a different path from theirs." I repeated his instructions.

The next day he gave me the tea mix, made from dried white rose petals, and the herbal bath mix, which smelled like a heady mixture of roses and rosemary.

The day after getting back to Berkeley, I went to several stores before finding beeswax candles. Selecting the photos of Matt and Heather was easy, since they are nestled into my bookcase in the den. In her photo, Heather is in her Apache uniform, with a bit of red hair showing below her specially contoured pilot's helmet, with a miniature computer screen covering her right eye. (She once told me the hardest part of learning to fly was training one eye to look in the computer eyepiece and the other to stare ahead.) She's wearing no makeup, and her freckles are visible, as is one blue eye. The photo should be on a kick-ass Army recruiting poster.

The framed photo I chose of Matt is actually two photos pieced together. As usual, he's wearing a long-sleeved, red-checked shirt, jeans, brown leather vest, and a gray-green wool hat with a brown leather band. In the mid-1990s we were in Lourdes,

France, a popular site for Catholic pilgrimages, and I asked him to stand next to a sign that read "Adoration Perpetuelle." But he wasn't satisfied with my choice of him as the focus of my secular adoration. He placed a photo of me on the other side of the sign, gluing the two together in a pre-Photoshop composition. On the photo, in ink, he drew an arrow on the sign pointing my way.

The first Friday morning I set a red-for-passion candle next to each photo on my bedroom dresser. I was comforted every time I walked into the room and glanced at the display. I lit the candles around nine o'clock, got into bed, and read until I fell asleep. When I woke up in the morning, the candles were still burning low. I put the green candles up the next day, even though I wouldn't burn them until Tuesday. Over the next four days, I looked at the photos and candles multiple times and again felt peaceful, meditating on what the color green stood for: spring, grass, growth, regeneration, resumption of life. On Tuesday I lit the candles at bedtime and watched them burn as I read, not wanting to fall asleep and miss a single glowing minute. Again I woke up to find the candles still burning. I repeated the ritual on the following Friday, lighting the path for Matt, Heather, and me with the golden candles. And I performed my last morning tea-drinking and face-washing rituals as well.

I left the golden candle remains on my dresser-shrine, next to the picture frames, for a few days, lamenting the end of the three-part ceremony. I felt at peace in a way I hadn't expected. Two additional unexpected things occurred. Several of my friends, who didn't know about my candle ceremony, commented they found me calmer and more relaxed than usual. "You're different," one friend said. "I don't know what it is. I can't explain it. You seem enthusiastic and quiet at the same time. And rested." I knew what she meant—I felt it too.

The other unanticipated by-product of my trip to Peru was the improvement in my sleep. I'd always had trouble sleeping through the night, especially in recent years. It was not unusual to fall asleep for a couple hours, wake up, and remain awake from two until four or five in the morning; this happened, on average, three or four times a week. Sleep aids were the unwanted antidote to too many sheet-thrashing nights. After the trip to Peru, I fell asleep and stayed asleep almost a hundred percent of the time. I don't know what happened. Was it Theo's helping me build a bridge between my conscious and unconscious selves by trekking through the energy fields of the majestic Andes, washing my face with invigorating herbs, and burning a rainbow of candles that cast their glow on those I loved and will always love? Apparently, whatever and however, passion, rebirth, and illumination suffused my inner being. Mysteriously, inexplicably, unexpectedly.

13

"CUP OF KINDNESS"

(Emmylou Harris)

The effects of Theo's commandment to burn the three sets of sacred candles stayed with me for the next year and more. My soul was calmed, and heart had connected with head. With the advent of the 2017 year-end holidays, which seemed to arrive the minute Halloween was over and to reach Mach 1 speed as the Thanksgiving dishes were piling into the dishwasher, I ignored the tinsel and colored lights and focused on the joy of giving something small, usable, and disposable to close friends. It wasn't like past Christmases with Matt and Heather when I concocted herb vinegars and oils and crafted festive table centerpieces, door wreaths, and candles. But for the first time in fifteen years, I enjoyed buying ready-made presents for people whose friendship I prized. Schedules permitting, we exchanged gifts over lunch or dinner, toasting our connectedness. My life felt richer than I'd expected it could be again.

The month was also filled with making preparations for a medical trip to the Dominican Republic. The cervical cancer prevention group I'd worked with for six years had folded when the founder and executive director retired. When no one emerged to carry on her work, I found a volunteer opportunity to fill the gap: Partners for Rural Health in the Dominican Republic, an organization associated with the University of Southern Maine's College of Nursing and Health Professions. For over twenty years, the PRHDR contingent had gone to the Dominican Republic twice a year for two weeks at a time, setting up pop-up clinics in churches and schools in the northeast, between coastal Puerto Plata and inland Santiago. Traveling by truck and, when necessary, on foot, teams of nursing school professors, students of nursing and physical and occupational therapy, volunteer doctors, nurses and nurse practitioners, dentists, pharmacists, physical therapists, interpreters, and nonmedical helpers headed to fifteen or twenty villages. They treated locals without health care for the unholy trinity of chronic diabetes, hypertension, and asthma, as well as for non-chronic headaches, back pain, joint problems, flu, scabies, parasites, infections, and a number of other complaints.

My decision to go for this new adventure prompted me to bone up on new terminology (unnecessary, as it turned out, but at least I added the words for gall bladder [*vesícula*] and spleen [*bazo*] to my vocabulary). And I stimulated the Bay Area economy by going to REI for the non-holiday items on my shopping list: mosquito netting and repellant, a solar shower bag, anti-diarrheal tablets, power bars, and dried fruit and nuts.

The volunteer materials warned us to expect mediocre food, uncomfortable lodging, and hot, rainy weather. "I don't know about this," I confided to close friends. "Most of the people on this trip will be nursing students, kids in their twenties. I'll be one of the oldsters—maybe the oldest." I'd never been with a group bigger than twenty and there would be at least sixty of us from the US, with a dozen more Dominicans joining us once we arrived. "It's going to be a zoo. Grand Central Terminal in the Caribbean boonies." Other concerns I kept to myself: Would we talk politics? Would we have anything in common, other than the work? And, besides eating bad food and sleeping three to a small room in bunk beds covered in mosquito netting, there would be frequent electrical outages, no Wi-Fi, and intermittent water in the bathrooms, cold to tepid at best. We were told to anticipate an array of bedroom companions including ants, roaches, spiders, centipedes, mosquitoes, and possibly bedbugs.

"It'll only be two weeks," I told my closest girlfriends. "If it doesn't work out, I'll keep looking." Or I might not. Hadn't I aged out of this kind of adventure? I liked warm showers, air conditioning, bug-free accommodations, and a watertight ceiling overhead. Nevertheless, I filled out the volunteer application, got references attesting to my ability to function without creature comforts, and visited Kaiser's injection clinic to get my shots and tuberculosis screening. I filled the prescription for malaria pills and lamented the lack of vaccines or cures for Zika, dengue, and chikungunya.

Three days after New Year's 2018, I arrived at Puerto Plata airport, met by a driver who took me to our quarters at a Catholic retreat center in the village of Lajas. The Dominican Republic is a tourist magnet, celebrated for dancing, *merengue* music, baseball, magnificent beaches, and stunning resorts, but our group saw nothing of this. As we set out each morning, we passed through villages of unpainted wood and cement shacks with outhouses and piles of garbage, debris, and underbrush lining the sides of muddy, potholed roads.

In contrast with the surroundings, the people were colorful, lively, friendly, and eager to engage. They called out to us heartily in a mix of Spanish and limited English. We responded in kind, in Spanish ranging from fluent down to enthusiastic, if wordless, waves and nods. Smiles and an "*Hola. Cómo está?*" from a first-year high school course went a long way. Housewives sat in front of their homes at small tables, selling a single block of cheese sliced on request, a few avocados, or slices of freshly baked coconut bread, smelling of cinnamon, which we bought for snacks. Nestled between the family dwellings was the occasional darkly lit *colmado*, usually a small hut where beer, chips, coffee, sodas, and lottery tickets were sold, as well as cabbages and heads of lettuce, to be sliced into smaller wedges and wrapped in newspaper. We bought drinks and munchies for our after-work social gatherings.

Within two days, I realized my fretting about the likelihood of physical discomforts was unfounded. Yes, there were electrical outages and scarce shower water, but who cared? The only thing that might have been unbearable—bedbugs—hadn't appeared.

The daily schedule rarely changed: my roommates and I awoke at six fifteen, deciding who would emerge first from the mosquito netting and find out if we had shower water. After breakfast at seven, we formed into teams and loaded the trucks with the day's provisions: folding chairs, bins of supplies, medications, lab tests, vitamins for children and adults, and patient files. If it was raining, we put on our well-used ponchos and took care not to slip as we carried our bulky cargo in the downpour. The second challenge was unloading and carrying the bins and paraphernalia, especially on hilly, muddy terrain. At times, some team members got out of the trucks and walked part of the way, with supplies in their backpacks, to visit patients unable to come to us. Occasionally a road was impassable, with trees blocking the way.

One day a small group crossed a river where a bridge had washed out. After jumping from stone to stone, they returned drenched but laughing, with mud-heavy sneakers and soaked pants.

At each location we set up eight or ten medical stations in a single room, each station staffed by a student nurse, a supervising nurse or nurse practitioner, and an interpreter. A roving doctor or two, a pharmacist, an intake receptionist, and a clinic doorkeeper rounded out the complement of personnel. All day patients flowed in, seated on church pews or squeezed into children's chairs. Even at the best of times, it was hard to hear. When rain pounded for hours on the corrugated metal roofs, the din made it impossible to tell who was saying what to whom.

Finding a quiet corner for intimate conversations or private examinations was a challenge. One woman for whom I was interpreting wanted to discuss sexual abuse and insisted on leaving the clinic to talk on the side of a school, next to the aromatic cement outhouse. On another occasion, four of us held our still wet ponchos around a middle-aged female patient lying on a narrow bench. Her complaint of abdominal pain prompted the nurse to ask her to remove part of her clothing, so she could check for pelvic abnormalities. "No, I have a better idea," the patient said, and gently took my poncho from me and spread it over herself. We blushed with embarrassment that she'd devised a far better strategy for privacy than we had.

Evenings we explored the area outside Fusimaña, our retreat center. We shared the puddle-rich, rutted *caminos* with friendly dogs we were instructed not to pet, dogs whose eyes and parasite-bloated stomachs showed they could use a pat, a meal, a bath, a trip to the vet, and a caring home. It was torture to keep my distance and let them go unattended. But we'd been counseled that we were there to help the people and not animals, who have nothing in common with our pampered pets back in the States. If they were famished, sick, or dying, that was just life in the Dominican Republic, as it is in the other countries where I've been a medical interpreter. Ignoring the dogs running the streets and the cats hanging around the *colmados* was the hardest part of every day.

We also kept our eyes on the traffic, sucking in our breath each time motorcycles, cars, and trucks whizzed around a blind curve, with a rare strip of sidewalk to run to for safety. We'd learned the Dominican Republic was reported by the World Health Organization to be the most dangerous country for road safety in the Western Hemisphere. Our knowledge was more than anecdotal: we saw this firsthand in clinic, each time the student nurses dressed the wounds of victims of motorcycle accidents and the physical therapy students adjusted their prostheses and provided them with crutches.

The days we spent working together in our jerry-rigged clinics felt like I was in church or at least my idea of what church should be like. It was about service, rather than sermons. It involved a collection of missionaries, not money. My two roommates from Maine, one a nurse and the other a call center manager from L.L. Bean, were perfect congregants: committed, lively, adventurous, engaged, flexible, and kind. Every night we exchanged stories of how the day's work had gone. We talked about our families and friends back home, bonding like sorority sisters. And we giggled about how we'd met our husbands (both Lisa and I were divorced from our first husbands and had juicy stories about how we met our second husbands). The twenty-year age difference between them and me went unnoticed, except obliquely when they remarked, "We can't stay up with you. Don't you get tired?"

The same level of bonding developed among all the American and Dominican volunteers, who ranged from high school age interpreters, to student nurses in their twenties to fifties, to retired medical and nonmedical workers in our sixties and seventies. As we merged into new teams, we formed working relationships organically, fluidly, instantaneously. The student nurses poured their souls into their work, caring for people whose health needs would have gone untreated had it not been for our organization. The group members, connecting with people from an environment so different from our own, increased, however modestly, the world's supply of good will.

I felt stripped of superfluous trappings, in touch with the essence of what matters in life, close to my skin, and accepted into others' skins and lives. I felt grateful, weightless, brushed by countless pairs of angel wings, not only those of the American and Dominican medical volunteers, but by the women who prepared food for us in the *comedor*, where we ate meals that were far better than we'd expected, and the van drivers who transported us to our daily clinics-to-be.

Our relationships with the patients were equally positive. As they left the clinic with their exam results and filled prescriptions, they hugged us and said, "*Gracias por todo, amigas*. Thank you for everything, my friends." This refrain was often followed by, "*Nos vemos pronto, si Dios quiere*. We'll see one another soon, God willing." The Dominicans' manner of leavetaking was gracious: they grasped us by the wrist and the lower part of the forearm and stroked gently, a movement that seemed more embrace than handshake.

Toward the end of our mission, I was assigned to a team making home visits to invalid patients for the entire day, working for the first time with a student nurse named Amber. Our driver dropped us off at the home of Ramona, an eighty-four-year-old woman with a long history of diabetes and diabetes-related neuropathy. After reviewing Ramona's file, Amber introduced herself. She spoke softly to the older woman, making visual contact in a calm, focused way that took my breath away. They seemed to be communicating in the same language, and not through me. I felt my voice coming from inside Amber's mouth, a mystical feeling I'd never experienced before. Amber proceeded with a few questions about Ramona's medications and pain level and then said, "Señora Ramona, tell me why you have that large bandage on your left big toe." *"Señora Ramona, dígame por qué se ha puesto la venda en el dedo grande del pie izquierdo,"* I repeated while Amber unwrapped the bandage.

Ramona responded she'd been asleep the previous week and a rat had chewed off the tip of her toe. She hadn't awakened. Ramona continued, "The next morning, my daughter helped me dress and pointed to my toe. It was bleeding." Ramona's daughter had used soap and water to clean the area and bandaged the wound.

Unruffled, Amber cleaned the toe with medicated solution, applied ointment, and consulted with the supervising nurse regarding the best antibiotic to heal the wound and stem the infection. "Watch me closely," she counseled, and I echoed her, "*Míreme bien.*" Amber showed Ramona's daughter how to dress the wound with the supplies we would leave behind and then continued the exam—Señora Ramona's other leg was ulcerated and required treatment. Amber ended by asking Ramona about her documented hypertension and back pain and then provided medications.

After attending to Ramona, Amber examined Ramona's two daughters, both in their fifties. Their files indicated they shared their mother's diagnoses of chronic diabetes and hypertension. Before leaving Ramona's home, Amber again asked each of them, "Do you have any more questions for me? Is there anything else you want to tell me?" They indicated they were done and thanked us for coming. As we left, Amber hastened to add, "Remember, we'll be back in six months." "*Recuerden—volveremos dentro de seis meses*," I repeated.

As we walked along the road to the next home visit, I took Amber aside and told her quietly, "I am so glad to have been your voice today. You were so caring and competent. It was an honor to work with you. If and when the time comes, I want you for my nurse." I was saying this to a twenty-six-year-old, someone I'd expected to have little in common with.

"I can't believe we didn't work together until today. I wish I'd worked with you every day," Amber responded. I wished the same, except then I wouldn't have worked with the other fine young people in the other villages on the other days of our mission.

Few of our patients approached the condition of Señora Ramona, but she was not alone. I worked with another woman with equally advanced diabetes, whose suppurating wounds attracted buzzing insects that stuck to her ulcers and who, like Ramona, couldn't feel her leg and didn't know the insects were there.

The patient in the direst physical condition was an elderly Haitian man. I heard about him at the end of the day when the team of volunteers returned from making home visits. They had hiked up a hill on a dirt path leading to the shack of a couple in their eighties. The bedridden man was blind, emaciated, and naked, covered in ants as he lay on a bare mattress of an unknown color. He had hypertension and diabetes. They couldn't leave medications for him because he couldn't understand how to take them. His half-blind wife had dementia, hypertension, and a heart condition. The team did what they could for the couple. They washed and dressed the husband, shook out the ant-infested mattress, and took his vital signs. They checked the wife's vital signs as well, but again couldn't prescribe medications because, like her husband, she didn't understand the instructions for taking the prescriptions for the assorted conditions she had. The team of five walked back down the hill without saying a word. Two of them wept.

The following evening I spoke with the nurse who'd described the visit with the Haitian couple. I asked how the students were doing. "They're processing it," she answered. "Most of them aren't talking about it; they've never seen anything like this. I haven't either." She continued, her eyes watering, "We emptied our backpacks and left everything we could: water, soft drinks, trail mix, and fruit. Even chewing gum." Over the weekend several volunteers dropped off bags of food and an envelope of money at the couple's home, a shack built of scrap wood with newspaper stuck in the cracks in the walls and ceiling to keep out the torrents of rain.

Even when tempted to break into tears at the description of unimaginable poverty, or to vomit at the sight of insects sticking to oozing wounds, I was grateful for the chance to be out of my element, to help on whatever microscopic scale I could. And thankful for how we worked together, each one of us contributing to the whole. It was, I thought, a miracle. However impoverished, gnawed, ulcerated, or ant-covered an individual was, we could do something about it. We could engage in an act of grace.

Another opportunity for grace, this one in four-legged form, surfaced on the fourth day of our stay. A three-pound, four-ounce black puppy with brown paws, a brownish-white chest and a wagging black tail bounced up the stairs into our makeshift clinic. The open-air church in Lajas de Yaroa was abuzz with patients and medical volunteers. When I saw the tiny female dog, between five and six weeks old, make her way up the cement steps, occasionally stumbling, I ignored her. Out of the corner of my eye, I glimpsed her visiting with clinic staff for a half hour, moving from station to station, and then tottering back down the steps to the unpaved road. She walked and bounced at the same time. Twice motorcycles sped by, missing her by inches. Still I looked away, until a young boy picked her up and she wiggled out of his arms, fell to the ground, and began howling in pain. She tried to walk and couldn't, and the howls continued. The boy hadn't dropped her intentionally, but neither he nor anyone in the street cared that she was injured. No one lifted a finger to comfort her. A car was coming down the road.

I left my station, flew down the steps, and picked her up. The howling turned into whimpering. I wiped off the dust and mud from her flanks and muzzle as she squirmed in my arms. She licked me once, then repeatedly. At that point I determined I would not leave her there. She would not die in the mud and dirt.

I brought her into the church, and a nurse, on break at the moment, took her from me, defying the clinic rules and holding the pup on her lap, so I could return to interpreting. As the afternoon went on, the nurse continued to hold the dog, and I checked with patients in the clinic and people on the road, to determine if she belonged to anyone. Nobody wanted her; she'd been dumped on the road several weeks earlier, an unwanted stray, eyes barely open. When codirector Doctor Cindy, who ultimately noticed the nicely recovered pup, approached me and asked what I was planning to do, she reminded me gently but firmly, "Sallie, you can't take the dog back to the center. You need to leave it here. We're here for the people."

My response was equally gentle and equally insistent, "I know I can't take her back to the center." Tears streamed down my face as I continued, "I'm sorry to break the rules. Cindy, I know we're here for the people. But I can't leave the dog here. I won't leave her here."

Cindy put her hand on my arm and said softly, "I understand. But she can't go back with us to the center, not even for tonight."

"I'll figure it out," I countered quietly. "But I will not let this dog die."

Dominican twins Jinet and Gina, volunteer fourth-year medical students, saw the worry on my face and approached, "*¿De qué están hablando? ¿Qué pasa? Todos están tan serios*." "What are you talking about? What's going on? You're all so serious."

When I explained I intended to rescue the puppy, but couldn't take her back to our retreat center, they called their mother. Within five minutes, Jinet told me, "Mami will take her for you. She's happy to." After work, we drove to the twins' house, where their mother, Noris, would keep the pup while I plotted the next steps. By then we had removed over seventy ticks from the irresistible three-pounder. Later that evening, at the center, a nurse I barely knew told me about an animal rescue site two hours away and gave me the number of Judy, the Canadian woman who ran the shelter. A truck driver agreed to take me there. My plan was to get Judy to find the dog a safe home with a local resident or put her in quarantine and I'd return to adopt her. Two days later, I retrieved the puppy from the twins' mother. When I got to the shelter, Judy said she didn't know anyone who was looking for a dog. "The puppy will need to get her shots over the next two months and then be quarantined for an additional month. You're probably looking at three months," she estimated. "I charge eight dollars a day for boarding, and her visa will be about twenty dollars plus airfare to send her to you in California. You won't need to fly back." I nodded.

The following evening Judy called to say the puppy—by then I'd temporarily named her Patas Sucias (Dirty Paws) or Suci for short—had been examined by a local veterinarian who deemed her physically healthy and sound of body and temperament. "The vet says she'll be better off in the States, and he'll provide paperwork to get her through immigration channels here and in Miami," Judy assured me. "You don't have to leave her here with me. She can go home with you." Six days after racing down the church steps to pick up a tiny howling creature, I flew home with a small pet carrier under the seat in front of me.

Back in California, I christened the puppy Grace, in honor of my entire experience in the Dominican Republic. Her name reflects the many moments of grace we shared with the people who helped us and whom we helped. And as a *recuerdo*, a souvenir, of my visit, I had the black-and-brown mutt, soon to have clean paws, a glossy coat, and a parasite-free intestinal tract. Along with Grace, I brought back a heart overflowing with joy, fuller than I thought it could ever be again, and made a promise to return to the Dominican Republic the following January.

14

"I CAN SEE CLEARLY NOW"

(Johnny Nash version)

Every year as the smell of autumn began to fill the air, I started to anticipate the soul flattening that occurred as the days got shorter and the year inched toward November, the month of Heather's birthday and my once-favorite holiday, Thanksgiving, and then charged toward Christmas, only to be followed ten days later by January 4th, the anniversary of Matt's and Heather's deaths. Their chairs at my dining room table were emptiest then, and I stopped making holiday dinners or wanting to share them with others. My preference was to take long walks and go to the movies alone on those once-festive occasions. Nevertheless, Matt's daughters always invited me to family gatherings. Often I showed up, but it was difficult to be there without him. There were parts of Matt in each of them, and I mourned his absence. At the same time, I was glad life went on for these exceptional young women and yearned to stay a part of their lives. As a compromise to the traditional gift-giving, I organized a new holiday: a three-day family weekend as their early Christmas present, scheduling it in October or early November, before dark-cloud time set in.

The Haiken family outings continue to this day, attended by my four stepdaughters, two granddaughters, young grandson, and me. Over the years, we've booked places all around Northern California. One requirement is that the cabins have good-sized kitchens, so we can prepare group breakfasts and dinners. They must be dog-friendly in an area with plenty of hiking options, and must have space for crafts projects, which have included macramé, driftwood hangings, and decorated stones. We talk, cook, eat, and laugh. And we craft while assorted husbands and husband-equivalents read, do crossword puzzles, and roll their eyes at our enthusiastic outbursts ("Look how Melia painted this rock to look like a fried egg and bacon!"). Being outdoors in the golden autumn afternoons with family, human and canine, is restorative beyond measure.

So the holidays got easier, as did the rest of my life, especially since my heart-expanding Sacred Valley trip. I wanted to keep letting the light and lightness through. My gratitude for close friends, health, financial security, and meaningful volunteer work with Rotarians had grown. I didn't want to backslide. But I needed a PASTRAMI boost. After a year of not finding Eureka Man, my energy was running low. I needed a kick in the pants.

Now, you can't live in Berkeley without hearing about life coaches. A coach plots out the steps to help a counselee reach her preidentified goal, rather than exploring the patient's past and underlying motivations for her dysfunctional behavior as a therapist would. For the most part, the life coach takes the counselee's word for what she wants to target: how to get her dream job, how to develop a plan for a rewarding retirement, how to balance work and family pressures, or how to find love. I wanted a coach, not a shrink.

I contacted Bill Say from among the many Berkeley-centered possibilities I Googled. According to his bio, he had a Master's in psychology, was a Processwork Diplomate, and had coached and taught in a number of university, community, and health settings. He'd run support groups and workshops and done private coaching for twenty-five years; his website said he was skilled in addressing issues of life direction and meaning (down my alley) and relationship issues (ditto). I liked everything I read in his Yelp reviews, with clients describing him as "dedicated, sensitive, engaging, motivating, grounded, and mindful." In our phone conversation, he came across as calm, open, and confident.

In our first session, I told Bill about myself in general and specifically about my two goals: I wanted his help in moving PASTRAMI forward and, at the same time, in appreciating my life exactly as it was. When I returned for our second session, I was impressed Bill had carefully reviewed the PASTRAMI site and taken notes to help him frame his questions. "What does a rewarding life mean to you? What does it look like?" he asked at the start of the session. When I told him that it meant being in a loving relationship and not feeling alone and empty, he followed up with, "Do you still feel connected to Matt and Heather? Because you can lose the person, but not the sense of feeling connected." I told him about the ceremony in Cusco and how the three-part candle ritual following my return to California had eased the paralyzing pain of my lost connection to them.

"You've told me about working hard to organize your life so as to find meaning in it, but it's still not multidimensional enough," he quickly replied. "I'm struck by how logical you are and yet profoundly emotional about what you love." As I listened to Bill, I felt understood. He continued, "These men you're telling me about who didn't ask anything about you . . . they weren't meeting you." But Bill was meeting me, in a way no one had since Matt.

At our next visit, Bill wanted to try something different. He'd heard me describe the endless pre-PASTRAMI coffee dates. "You say you can't take much more. It wears you down. Why stay so long if you know after ten minutes it's not going to work?" he asked gently, but firmly. He suggested we role play, telling me to talk to him as if he were the no-way guy. "Tell me it was nice to meet me, but it won't work for you. Are you up for that?"

I nodded.

Bill started by saying hello, then went on nonstop about himself. As he chattered, I made a couple of stuttering attempts to stop him, but he kept at it, describing in excruciating detail how much he enjoyed playing golf and how frustrating it had been since his friend and favorite golf partner left town. When he saw I wasn't succeeding in getting him to stop, Bill interrupted his monologue, "If you can't stop him, give yourself an escape route. When you decide time's up—after fifteen, twenty, or twenty-five minutes—excuse yourself to go to the bathroom. In the ladies' room, practice what you're going to say, and take a few deep breaths. Then come out and say good-bye."

We repeated the role play and, at the imaginary twenty-minute point, I interrupted him mid-yammering on about his love of golf. Without attempting a smooth segue, I announced, "I'm going to leave now. You have lots to offer and to share with the right woman. But our interests are different; we're not looking for the same things. Thank you for meeting me. I wish you the best."

"Good—you didn't go into logic mode and explain or provide a list," Bill complimented me. "Don't defend your decision to leave. You don't need to say how you're different and what you don't have in common," Bill said. But then, just as I thought we were done and I could pat myself on the back, he assumed a hurt look on his face and tried to suck me in. "Why do you think we're too different?" he asked. "I like being outdoors and I don't dislike travel. I think we could get along."

"I don't agree," I replied. "And, besides, you deserve someone who wants to be with you." I was so into the role playing that I stood up. I felt physically relieved as I moved toward the exit, and pleased when Bill reminded me, with an amused look on his calm face, "You didn't mention your biggest complaint. Did you realize I didn't ask you a single question? Was that on your mind? But it doesn't matter—you don't need to give reasons."

Our most moving coaching session occurred the week of Heather's forty-seventh birthday. I told him I'd expected this year would be easier because I'd gotten through September and October with relative ease, but then I'd taken a November nosedive and had again sought support from Pema Chodron's *When Things Fall Apart*. It wasn't so much that things were continuing to fall apart—it was that the pieces weren't coming back together.

He instructed me to play Feeling Sallie, who refused to accept his censure; he appointed himself to the role of Critical Sallie. "I miss them. I love them. I think I've accepted Matt's death and absorbed it, but I can't accept Heather's. I don't think I ever will." I continued with increasing energy in my voice, cutting Bill off when he said, "Get over it. You've had plenty of time to adjust."

"I have the right to feel this way. It's a feeling beyond pain." Twice Bill dropped the act, saying, "I can't even pretend to feel critical. You've persuaded me."

I felt vindicated. I wasn't being weak or self-indulgent. Liberated, lighter by half, I realized I had the right not to be over it. It was too much to be over.

Next, Bill had us switch roles and told me to be as hard on myself as I could.

"Let the past stay in the past. Get with the program," I heard my critical self say impatiently.

"No, it's not past," he answered. "My feelings are right now. I'm going to let my feelings come up and give them their due. I am honoring my pain. I respect my pain."

I started crying.

"You're processing deep emotions," Bill told me gently. "Keep doing it. You will be grounded and wise. When you reach the deep knowing place, you will connect with a wonderful man."

I wanted to believe him, believe it was possible to get to that knowing place, and from there, to the connecting place. But I didn't know what steps to take, where the road map was to lead me in the right direction. I only knew I had to discover it inside myself. What I did know was that the longer I wept, the better I felt. Since Matt and Heather's deaths, crying had seemed like too light a way to express what I felt. It was putting a Band-Aid over a machete gash. I'd felt more like screaming in rage or jumping off a cliff. But now I was crying, and it felt healing.

For the next few days, I mulled over coach Bill's admonition to silence my critic if I wanted to be happy, basically to tell disparaging Steve to put a sock in it. For years I'd thought a lot about what being happy involved, and the difference between happiness, pleasure, and joy. I remembered how easy it used to be for me to recognize, in the moment, how happy I was. During Matt's occasional dark-cloud periods, especially early on, he called me "Rebecca of Sunnybrook Farm." "You're too happy," he would complain grumpily, as if I'd failed him in some way. "You haven't dealt with tragedy." He'd lost two of his closest boyhood friends, one in his late twenties and the other in his mid-thirties; one of his two sisters to cancer at age fifty; and his seventy-four-year-old father to a heart attack.

"That will change soon enough," I countered. "I'll lose some of the people I love. It's inevitable. Why does it annoy you that I'm happy?"

What would he say to the Sunnybrook Farm girl now?

"Sarah, I'm so sorry. You've had more than your share." And then he'd add, "*Mea culpa*," one of his favorite expressions. To his credit, he always apologized when he'd gotten out of line.

I've come to regard happiness and joy as the same thing. Pleasure, though, is a knock-off of joy, a crimped version of happiness, with discrete starting and stopping points. Click ON: I go to lunch with a friend and have fun. Click OFF: We say good-bye and go our separate ways. The good feeling ends, although the pleasant memory may linger in a diluted form, a gust of fresh wind that wafts in and then out. The window is shut, the door is closed. Joy and happiness, on the other hand, are the breezes that continue throughout the day, from morning to night. And the next morning the caressing flow endures, uninterrupted.

Joy is what Matt was referring to when, six months after we met, he declared gently, "I never knew it could be like this. I move through my days in sweet air. I don't take this for granted."

Years later, reading an article about the chemistry involved in making French perfume, I discovered the word *sillage*. It refers to the trail of scent a woman wearing perfume leaves behind when she departs a room. It's the aromatic equivalent of a wake left by a boat in the water or a plane's trail of smoke in the sky. It reminded me of Matt's sweet air image.

In my post-Andes months, and especially during my sessions with Bill, I became increasingly aware that the *sillage* of pleasure was lasting longer and spreading over more territory. But the approach of Heather's birthday was still guaranteed to deliver a kick in the gut, as was seeing in the distance a tall, slender young woman with shoulder-length red hair. But hearing a treasured song playing over the radio or passing a man on the street wearing a hat like Matt's no longer triggered an emotional blow to the solar plexus. I not only listened to our Willie Nelson CDs, I sang along at top volume. Episodes of finite pleasure were more and more merging with continuing joy and happiness. I enjoyed spending time with friends and then going home to walk, garden, read, and play with my dogs. I went alone to movies, plays, and dinner out of choice, not desperation. It actually felt good to walk into my empty house after returning from a trip and yell to the dogs, "Hi, guys, I'm home." I got down on all fours on the rug, and we touched noses as I rubbed tummies and scratched butts. If it wasn't too dark, we went for a walk. A peaceful, calm homecoming. Canine friends weren't my number one choice to accompany me into the bedroom, but they provided joy to be sure.

I was still sleeping through most nights. I rarely employed my oft-practiced meditation techniques of slowly breathing in and out, while focusing on the spot between my eyebrows, to empty my conscious mind. I had no idea what had caused the dial on the zero-to-ten happiness meter to creep up from occasional pleasure to frequent joy. Was it hiking in the snowcapped mountains, breathless and exhausted at impossible altitudes, knowing it didn't matter that I'd never reach a single peak? Was it embedded memories of the shaman-anthropologist's feathers, bells, and rattles touching my outer body and inner soul? The effect of the candles that cast their glow so Matt and Heather could follow a path different from mine and I could love them from afar? Bill's coaching dexterity, weaving the threads of my Cusco experiences into a new pattern? It must have been all of it.

Bill often referred to "Andes Sallie" and shone a light on what she knew. He talked, inquired, and counseled; he encouraged and supported. He wondered out loud. His words "I wonder if" became my signal to listen carefully because I knew he was on to something. He reminded me, through conversations and role plays, that Andes Sallie was far wiser than Berkeley Sallie. Andes Sallie could point the way to what he called the deep knowing place. With Bill helping me, I climbed up and down, stumbled, caught my breath, got up, and focused my eyes on the peak ahead.

I was happy, healthy, and free. Feeling like a whole person after years of living with an amputation, I welcomed the sensation of a flow of fresh, calm water moving through me at an even pace. I didn't need the drama of a waterfall inundating body and soul, leaving me breathless. Most importantly, for the first time in sixteen years, I wasn't lonely.

15

"THE FIRST TIME EVER I SAW YOUR FACE"

(Roberta Flack version and
the reggae version by Marcia Griffiths)

Once again I took a break from PASTRAMI after little success finding a Candidate from the age-appropriate, unattached male population. I was considering dumping PASTRAMI entirely when my friend Marcia, who'd tried to connect me with meditation instructor David, called to propose a second Candidate: Bart, a retired physician and health care executive whose wife had died barely a year before, after a happy marriage of thirty-seven years.

I wasn't sure I was ready to consider a new PASTRAMI possibility quite yet, but Marcia was persuasive. She had worked for Bart at a health plan for eight years in Oregon in the early 1990s, when he was CEO of the company. "That was almost thirty years ago, and he's one of my dearest friends. He's the best boss I've ever had. Maybe the finest man I've ever known."

He seemed so apparently special that I felt a hopeful twinge in my stomach. (Sweet Pea: "Eureka Man might be showing up." Steve: "There she goes again, counting chickens.")

I resolved to keep expectations to a minimum. Besides, whether I liked him or not, he might feel nothing for me. Even if he did and we ended up going out, his wife had died too recently, and I did not need to be reminded what it felt like to dig and scrape yourself out of a seemingly bottomless abyss.

I asked Marcia to tell me how Bart was handling his wife's loss. "So far he's been hunkering down at home, grieving. Reading a lot and thinking. Jogging and going to the gym. Except for errands and yard work, he doesn't go out unless a friend suggests breakfast or lunch. He talks with friends on the phone, mostly when we call. He may or may not be ready to start going out. It's hard to know, but I can tell you it's worth a shot. He's wonderful."

I couldn't help contrasting Marcia's friend's way of handling his grief-burdened days with mine. Back then, I couldn't sit still or sleep. I was on the go constantly—anything to avoid being in a Matt-empty house, where everything carried memories of togetherness. Whenever I stopped spinning, the searing, stabbing pain intensified.

And here Marcia's friend was doing the opposite: spending his days lying low, staying inside, surrounded by furniture, photographs, plants, books, and music he and his wife had collected, living with echoes. What would be daily doses of salt in a wound for me was apparently comforting and consoling for him.

But there was more. "He has a dog." (Sweet Pea: "Bingo!" Steve: "A blended dog family. Yeah, that always works.")

Marcia's enthusiasm gradually overcame my resolve not to get excited. And life coach Bill had admonished me to keep my heart open, hadn't he? I would do just that.

"Yes, Marcia, I'd like to meet him," I heard myself say.

Marcia said, "I should tell you I don't see Bart ever leaving Portland for the Bay Area or for anywhere else for that matter. But you have the freedom to live in two places, and he's totally worth the effort. And Portland's wonderful."

I agreed with her about Portland. I'd been there a few times and had enjoyed it enormously. Besides, if we clicked, a commuting partnership sounded fine. I wasn't seeking one hundred percent togetherness. The insurmountable obstacle wasn't geography; it was his not being ready for a relationship. Before hanging up, she added a final caveat, "One last thing. I haven't told him about PASTRAMI. There's no way he would agree to meet you if he thought romance was the objective. There can be no mention of it. Agreed?"

I had no problem with that. It would be a relief not to be a contestant on an old folks' version of *The Dating Game.* Before hanging up, we talked about a likely date for the adventure, the sooner, the better. "Are you willing to go the next time I head up to Portland?" Marcia asked. "I'm hoping to see friends in early December, before the holidays. You could come along."

"Yes indeedy, sweetie," I answered. "I have a friend from high school in Michigan who lives there, and she's invited me over and over to visit. It would be great to see her, and I could meet your friend Bart on the same trip."

Sooner became later. It took four months from the time of Marcia's phone call till we could coordinate schedules. Holiday commitments and the trip to the Dominican Republic interfered. But finally we set a date for a rendezvous: she, husband Herb,

Bart, and I would meet for dinner at a downtown restaurant in their former hometown.

But now, after so much time, I wasn't sure I was still up for this.

Marcia called the week before our dinner to check in and update me about details of our meeting. "I gave him a little information about you. I told him you were our close friend and that we get together a lot in the Bay Area. I mentioned you're from Louisiana and a liberal like him. He liked that, your being Southern, without being—you know—'Southern.'" She told me where and when our dinner reservation was, adding, "I'd already told him I wanted him to choose a place he'd never been with his wife—one that didn't stir up memories. He didn't ask me any questions. And, in talking with him just now, he didn't seem to think it was odd that you were coming along with Herb and me."

I flew up to Portland two days early to hang out with my high school pal Harriet before the restaurant get-together. She was divorced and not seeing anyone, and the subject of men and romance didn't come up. Once or twice I almost mentioned the purpose of the dinner, but since the encounter might end up going nowhere, I decided against full disclosure. If the evening were a dud, I didn't need her to ask about it. "The less discussed the better," I told myself.

Mid-afternoon on my second day in Portland, I took a walk in Harriet's neighborhood. Ten minutes into the walk, I came across a woman vacuuming her car. When she saw me approach, she offered to unplug the cord stretched across the sidewalk and move it out of my way.

"Good grief, no. I'm fine," I responded. "Are you vacuuming because you have dogs?" She nodded yes, adding that, with the winter rain and drizzle, her dogs kept her car in a perpetually dirty mess. We started talking about our dogs; we discovered we had a mutual love of rescue dogs, and both of us were involved in rescue dog volunteer work. She also said she had once lived in the Bay Area and visited there frequently.

She continued vacuuming, and I continued accumulating FitBit steps. On my return, I made sure to walk by the house and write a brief note for my new acquaintance, with my name and cell phone number.

In less than an hour Shelley called to invite me to have a glass of wine the next day. "I told my husband about you. I said I wished I'd gotten your name and phone number. And then you swung by and left me the note. It was meant to be!"

The following afternoon, she opened the door with a welcoming smile. I asked to see her dogs, found out she had cats as well, and the love fest continued. We talked about San Francisco and Berkeley, both of which she knew well. Finally, she asked me why I was visiting Portland, and I told her about spending time with a pal, and then, to my surprise, I blurted out that I was to be introduced to a man at dinner that night.

"Who are you meeting?" Shelley asked, innocently enough. I had forgotten his last name, but told her he was a retired doctor and health care executive named Bart.

"Bart McMullan?" The look of incredulity on her face blended with her widening smile.

I nodded.

"My husband and Bart worked together—their offices were right next to each other," Shelley told me, grinning. "They know each other really well. Randy thinks the world of him," she said, grabbing her phone. "Randy, where are you?" she asked her husband when he answered. "You need to come home right this minute. Costco can wait. No, it's not an emergency, but come home. You are not going to believe this."

Within ten minutes, husband Randy was home, and we were being introduced. "Randy, this is Sallie, you know, she left the note. Guess who she's going to meet tonight? Bart McMullan."

The smile that spread over Randy's face mirrored Shelley's. "He's one of the finest men I've ever worked with."

"I can see you together," Shelley chimed in. "I can really see you together."

I walked back to Harriet's house, dazed by the coincidence of meeting Shelley and Randy and struck by their ringing endorsements of Marcia's opinion of how special Bart was and of the possible match we might make. Shelley's enthusiastic "I can really see you together" boded well for the evening. I dressed with more care than usual, evaluating the few outfits I'd brought. I wished I'd packed with a bit more pizzazz. I put on earrings I'd made from turquoise nuggets and silver findings from my bead store in Berkeley. I applied a rare layer of lipstick and a puff of face powder and checked the mirror more times than usual. There was still time to kill. I picked up a magazine, put it down, and picked it up again. The minutes dragged. After primping for the nth time, I picked up my iPhone to call Uber. I arrived fifteen minutes early for dinner.

When I entered the fashionable Headwaters Restaurant, it was bustling with the Friday after-work crowd of millennials enjoying designer cocktails at the gleaming bar. The hostess offered me a seat in the lounge to the right of the exposed kitchen, assuring me she'd notify me when my party arrived. I welcomed sitting down in the quiet, sedate room, reminiscent of a library reading room. I'm not good at waiting even under normal circumstances, and Shelley's enthusiasm added to my jitters. More was riding on this dinner, emotionally speaking, than I had imagined just a few hours earlier. I sank comfortably into an overstuffed armchair.

I watched the few other people in the lounge and impatiently tracked the minute hand on my watch. Twenty minutes passed. Marcia, Herb, and Bart should have arrived. When I approached the harried hostess directing the stream of patrons to their tables or to the bar, she was apologetic. She'd seated them ten minutes earlier and had forgotten to come for me. I strolled over to their table and explained why I was late. The three of them had already ordered cocktails and were in the midst of a lively conversation. Bart stood up to shake hands, and I took the empty seat to his left.

Bart was wearing a suede camel blazer and, under it, a light-colored shirt without a tie. I was struck by his soft Mississippi accent, his light blue eyes, and his sandy brown hair, free of gray for the most part. His slender face was clear and thoughtful, surprisingly boyish for someone my age. He was easily six feet tall and slim, possibly skinny—it was hard to tell under his jacket.

Within minutes of sitting down, my nervousness had disappeared. Marcia and Herb went out of their way to put me at ease, but it wasn't necessary. Bart seemed both familiar and new at the same time. He was engaged in all aspects of the conversation, leaning toward whoever was speaking, with a semi-smile on his face and his gentle blue eyes fully focused. His listening was three-dimensional, quietly physical, as he bent ever so slightly toward the center of the table to probe a remark, question a statement, or challenge a position. He never appeared to be thinking of what he would say next. When he did speak, he spoke quietly, exuding a calm confidence that prompted me to move closer to him to make sure I heard his low-decibel comments. I agreed with Marcia that he didn't need to talk much because when he did, it counted. I didn't want to miss anything. I wanted to hear more from this man who spoke volumes in so few words.

Marcia kept the conversation flowing. "Sallie, I was telling Bart I haven't seen you since you got back from the D.R. a couple of weeks ago, but that you've been sending me updates on your puppy. Show him the picture you sent me of her sitting on your lap on the plane." I mentioned how Grace had had over seventy ticks on her tiny body and had been treated for parasites three times. I recounted the three to four times a night I'd been taking her outside with attacks of explosive diarrhea. (Herb and Bart were both doctors and Marcia was a medical social worker, so topics like ticks, parasites, and diarrhea weren't off-limits at the dinner table.) More happily, I recounted how well my puppy was adjusting to life with an abundance of food and veterinary care.

The server came to ask what I wanted to drink, and we placed our food order. When I asked if anyone wanted to share a calamari appetizer with me, Bart answered with a two-syllable "ye-es." His accent released unexpected waves of nostalgia for my paternal grandparents' home in Opelika, Alabama, where my family spent part of every summer when I was a child. Bart's syllable-stretching, word-merging, slow-cadenced speech resonated with memories of hugs from loving relatives who gave us popsicles and sodas we weren't normally allowed to have, of walking barefoot on the hot sidewalk, and of climbing up on uncles' and aunts' laps. And, most happily, of stretching out on my grandparents' front porch swing, as my grandfather made up stories for my sister and me, and we watched lightning bugs flitting in the darkening evenings.

The waiter came by to check on us, which gave me the chance to ask for extra lemon on our appetizer. All my life I've been ridiculed for my love of lemon. I always request five wedges for a single glass of iced tea. I cook everything with lemon. So when the calamari arrived, I asked if I could squeeze lemon on both sides. "Ye-es," Bart replied, followed by, "Ah nevah met a lemon Ah didn't lahk." So he had a sense of humor as well as a heart-stopping accent. I was getting breathless. I smiled, touched by the feeling of home washing over me and bathing my heart.

I liked this man.

Over our entrees we talked about the Arlie Hochschild book *Strangers in Their Own Land,* documenting Dr. Hochschild's five years of research into the reasons conservative white working class Americans had seemed to vote against their own interests in recent elections. Part of our spirited discussion focused on Bart's and my knowledge and experiences of the Deep South. About this, Bart had much to say. "It's not about policy. It's personal. We Democrats think we can win with policy. We're wrong. The Democrats in Congress don't git it."

During the evening, I continued to be aware of Bart's listening skills: his head tilting forward, his eyes connecting with the person speaking at the time, talking without talking, communicating by listening. I was also aware of a growing urge on my part to touch his left arm, positioned just inches to my right. I considered brushing lightly against him as if by accident, but held back.

Throughout the two-hour dinner, I looked for signs of the deep grief of this long-married, newly widowed man. He seemed more healed than Marcia had described. He didn't seem to be covering up the dark side of his life. I didn't sense that spending time with him would strew a shitload of hazardous material in my emotional path. Bart was serious and thoughtful and at the same time lighthearted and open. How could I feel this way about someone I hadn't been alone with for five minutes? But I was one hundred percent certain I liked everything about him, his mind, his face, his spirit—and, as far as I could tell, his body.

Finally, over dessert, after we'd exhausted national political topics and snippets of Portland news of interest to the others, I recounted the story of my chance encounter with Shelley and Randy. We marveled over the improbability of a vacuum cleaner cord on the sidewalk leading to a chat about rescue dogs, leading to my leaving a note on their doorstep, leading to an invitation to wine, leading to the discovery of their friendship with Bart. Again, I felt a ridiculously premature connection to this man, who tried to shrug off Randy's statement, "He's one of the finest men I've ever known." He did this in an "aw shucks" way that reminded me of Jimmy Stewart. Given his boyish looks and lanky build, he even looked like Stewart a bit, mixed in with the more handsome Henry Fonda.

I had planned to take Uber back to Harriet's house after dinner, but Bart offered to drop me off on his way home. "It's no trouble at all. It's on my way," he assured me. When Bart pulled up in front of her house, I thanked him for the ride. He said, "I enjoyed meeting you," without much enthusiasm in his voice. I waited for him to add, "And I'd like to see you again." He didn't. I hoped he'd offer to walk me to the door, but he remained at the wheel. As I closed the door and turned to watch him pull away from the curb, I mulled over his succinct four-word farewell, "I enjoyed meeting you." I hoped that he might possibly, conceivably, improbable-though-it-might-seem, have meant it.

The next day Marcia told me Bart had sent her a follow-up email, "Enjoyed dinner. Thanks for inviting Sallie. Nice lady."

"He likes you," Marcia said. "He had a good time and was glad to meet you."

I was disappointed. For me, it was more than good. It had been a great dinner. More than great, it was close to spectacular.

A little subdued, I flew back to California. Back in Berkeley,

I wondered if there would be a next step. I called my favorite Love Liaison to discuss the situation. "I was going to call you later this morning, but you beat me to it," Marcia confided. "Bart called last night. Said he was glad to have met you. He tried to sound low key and noncommittal, but I know him." After a momentary hesitation, she added, "But you're going to have to take the initiative. He won't. I know he wants to see you again, but don't expect him to contact you."

I had two reactions. One was a neon fireball of excitement: he liked me. The other was a hard nut of frustration and annoyance: *I* would need to make a move? I was tired of being the one to make things happen. Hadn't Marcia and I done enough to arrange a successful first encounter with this stellar Candidate? I wanted him to pursue me, make it clear he found me desirable, let the pitty-pat in his heart kick into testosterone-fueled high gear. But if I wanted to see him again, it was up to me.

Serendipitously, Arlie Hochschild, whose book had triggered so much of our conversation, was speaking at Berkeley Rotary the month after our dinner date. I called Marcia to tell her I was sending an email to her, Herb, and Bart, inviting them to hear the presentation. My email included a special invitation, "If Bart is willing to take BART [the Bay Area Rapid Transit train] from the airport, I'd love to have him join us." I spent some time with the phrasing, wanting to achieve the perfect blend of playful, enthusiastic, and welcoming, but not too eager.

Marcia emailed back immediately, copying Bart. She and Herb would attend. Within a quarter of an hour, she called to tell me Bart had emailed her. "He thinks maybe you are just being nice to invite him," she said, amused. "I assured him you meant it and want him to come. He said he would." She continued with a note of mild irritation in her voice, "For years Herb and I have invited him to come visit us in the Bay Area, and he's never accepted. Now, minutes after getting your invitation, he's said yes. He's coming for you."

Within minutes, Bart emailed his response, "I'd like to come, but I'd like to see you more than just at the meeting. If I come and stay with Marcia and Herb, could we get together outside of Rotary?" I was heart-jumpingly, poppingly, out-of-my-skin elated. I wanted to write back, "*Yay*! A thousand times *yay*!" but with the self-restraint that I'd managed at the restaurant when I didn't touch his arm, I simply wrote, "Yes, I would like that. That would be nice. Am looking forward to seeing you." I held back adding, "I'm counting the days. I can't wait."

Once he'd accepted my invitation, we were on an e-roll, exchanging emails every other day and soon every day and then several times a day. I came to see his neighborhood through his descriptions of daily dog walks; I imagined him holding the leash of his regal white shepherd, heading home. I imagined walking with them both, talking as we passed the leash back and forth. (Sweet Pea: "Nice. Romantic. Walking, talking." Steve: "And picking up poop. Very romantic.")

Marcia soon heard from Bart that we'd been emailing daily. She called me, tickled. "Sallie, when Bart told me how frequently you two are emailing, I told him he could pick up the phone and call you in person." She laughed as she told me what he said: "'Huh. I didn't think of that.'" He emailed me later that day, asking if he could call me. We talked that evening and every evening after that. Short chats became half-hour calls and ultimately stretched to an hour. The emails continued.

From day one, whether via email, on the phone, or in person, music had been a constant topic of discussion. Bart had played saxophone in his high school band and also in two rock bands, one in high school and, decades later, one in Portland with a group of doctors in their forties. They called themselves "The Love Handles." I'd sung in church choirs throughout my childhood and in my high school choruses; as a graduate student, I sang and played folk music on my guitar in Berkeley coffee houses. I've never stopped singing.

We exchanged titles of songs of our favorite genres: rock and roll, folk, Motown, R & B, and country rock. The list was endless: Fats Domino, The Platters, The Temptations, The Everly Brothers, Elvis, Roy Orbison, Kris Kristofferson, Fleetwood Mac, John Denver, Joan Baez, Judy Collins, Leonard Cohen, Johnny Cash, Willie Nelson, Bob Seger, Steve Goodman, Rod Stewart. Bart introduced me to Sammi Smith and Betty Everett and the marvelous gone-too-soon Eva Cassidy. I shared Johnny Adams and John Hiatt with him.

One afternoon I clicked on an email from Bart; it was blank except for the subject line, "The First Time Ever I Saw Your Face"—Roberta Flack. Marcia was right that Bart was a man of few words, but oh so wrong when she said he didn't manage to say much. I sent back an email with only a subject line, "Unchained Melody"—The Righteous Brothers. He followed up with "When You Say Nothing at All"—Alison Krauss and "Lay Down Beside Me"—Alison Krauss and John Waite. He also sent me "I Never Thought I Could Love Again"—Dan Hill.

For every song he sent, I sent one back with the title of a says-it-all song in the subject line and no text. Johnny Adams's "There's Always One More Time" and Iceman Jerry Butler's "For Your Precious Love" were the titles that said best everything I wanted to say to Bart. It doesn't get any better than Iceman.

Bart got into the habit of sending photographs of his rear deck overlooking the backyard. He took them from his bedroom at night, with the moon shining through the trees, and in the morning at sunrise. I responded in kind, with shots of my yellow and peach-colored roses, my dogs at play, and cartoons I found in the daily paper. We were welcoming each other into our homes, our gardens, our lives, and providing personal details, large and small: the thoughts we ruminated over, books we read, food we ate, walks we took, dogs we cared for, friends we saw. Our connection grew fluidly and naturally.

In one of our early calls, Bart wanted to know, "Why did you name your older dog McGee?" I told him I always name my dogs after songs, so I can sing their name-songs to them. "McGee is named for 'Me and Bobby McGee.'"

"But why did you choose it? It's one of my favorites." I hesitated before telling him the real reason, worrying he might be put off by my excessively personal revelation. "Because it says it all: 'Freedom's just another word for nothing left to lose.'"

"I understand," he drawled. "It's the same with me. That's why I asked."

I hadn't told him about Matt and Heather, but knew Marcia had. Inviting him to break through my wall of self-protectiveness, I continued, "After my husband and daughter died, I had nothing left to lose. I lost everything I loved." I stopped, but he said nothing. "I always expected to lose my husband because of our age difference, but not so soon. I never thought I would lose my daughter. So that's why he's McGee."

Instead of being at a loss for words, Bart responded, "I felt that way when Patti died." I stayed silent, as he continued, "I expected I'd be alone for the rest of my life and was at peace with it. I figured I'd been lucky up till then and didn't deserve more." His low voice grew lower, "I was fine. I'd had my fair share. I felt that way until I met you. I don't feel that way anymore."

I felt a surge of gratitude and wonderment. Had we truly become this close in less than a month, through email and phone calls? We hadn't seen each other since our first dinner, and even then we hadn't been alone. It seemed inconceivable to have broken through the awkwardness of getting to know each other, of filing down the rough, sharp edges of unfamiliarity from hundreds of miles apart. We'd shared our losses without being crippled by them. Bart wasn't dragging me through toxic dust; I wasn't reliving the excruciating weeks and months and years after Matt became ashes in a wooden box and again after Heather's body was placed in a coffin and buried in Arlington, Virginia. In spite of it all, here we were, holding hands and embracing through the ether, affirming love in the midst of ruin, reveling in the promise of good things to come. We still could see the black hole each of us had been mired in, but little by little the distance between where we were standing and the blackness below us had increased. Our perspective had changed and, with it, the future.

Time moved at a snail's pace, with two weeks remaining before Bart's visit to Berkeley. I was in New Orleans, visiting a dear friend with a terminal illness. Each evening, when Bart and I talked on the phone, he built up my sagging spirits and provided medical counsel. Several days before my planned return to California, he said he wished we were going to see each other sooner. "I know the two weeks will pass, but time is dragging," he sighed. On the spur of the moment, I suggested I fly from New Orleans to Portland rather than heading back to San Francisco. That would eliminate the wait, and we could have private time together before joining Marcia and Herb as a foursome. (Steve: "You're acting like a lovestruck teen." Sweet Pea: "And about time. Go for it!")

Bart met me at the Portland airport. I exited security and looked around eagerly for him, thinking he might be delayed or still looking for a parking spot. Then I saw him stand up from a chair and close the book he'd been reading. My heart began pounding. I'd been thrilled and terrified during the five-hour flight, worried that my load of expectations would be too heavy for us to carry. What if we didn't get along as well face-to-face as we had at a distance? What if we had little to say to one another and came to regret this whole venture?

But as he moved toward me, I knew we would be all right. He looked at me gently with his lovely serious face and lit-from-within blue eyes and just said, "Hello." He put his arms around me. I stretched up to put my arms around his neck and touch his shoulders. He was taller than I remembered, and I felt surprisingly small and protected. He gave me the most dangerously and sizzlingly stunning kiss of my life. We leaned into each other, kissing, and not speaking for several minutes, as people walked past us with their luggage.

As we walked to the parking lot, holding hands, Bart dragged my roller bag. "Don't be afraid, but my dog will lunge at you from the back of the car," Bart warned. "She's harmless, but seventy-five pounds of white fur barking and leaping at you can be scary." I stood my ground, grateful for the glass on the hatchback door. Once he opened the side door to put in my luggage, she ceased barking, sniffed me, and settled down. Driving home, we said little and listened to the fifties music playing on the radio. I'm pretty sure I rested my left hand on his leg.

A vase of roses on the sofa table was the first thing I saw as we walked into his living room. I gasped at the beauty of a dozen perfect flowers tinged in apricot and brandy. "They're for you," he said, kissing me again. He lit a fire and turned back toward the sofa where I was seated. "Would you like a glass of wine? Marcia said I should have sauvignon blanc for you."

We moved to the carpet to be closer to the fireplace, leaning against the sofa, drinking wine, and celebrating my spur-of-the-moment decision to fly from Louisiana. We talked easily, a bit about my luck with the flight change from New Orleans and his chat with Marcia earlier in the day. "I told her you were flying up, and she seemed surprised. Disapproving even. She's probably thinking we're off the charts."

Bart asked what I wanted to do during our time together in Portland.

"I don't care," was my immediate reply. "I'd like to see the city, but mostly I want to talk and listen to music with you. And walk the dog and see your neighborhood." The panic I'd felt on the plane had given way to total ease. The more we talked, the more natural it felt.

After a while, Bart saw I was flagging and covering up a yawn. He asked if he should take my roller bag and backpack to the downstairs guest room he'd readied for me. It sounded to me like he was asking about more than moving my luggage.

"No, I'd like to stay with you," popped out of my mouth.

"What does 'want to stay with you' mean?"

"It means to sleep with you."

"And what does that mean?"

With the fire still burning, I kissed him, took his hand, and simply said, "Let's not be teenagers." We got up from the carpet and walked to his bedroom, where the moon was shining through the windows. We called the dog and invited her to follow us.

16

"THERE'S ALWAYS ONE MORE TIME"

(Johnny Adams version)

The following week, I met Bart at the Oakland airport. The kiss we exchanged was less intense than that first kiss in Portland, but it was comfortable and familiar. Unfortunately, it was also shorter, since the traffic guard policing the drop-off lane was yelling at me to move along or she would issue me a ticket. Bart was in the Bay Area for four nights, spending the first night at Marcia and Herb's house and the rest of his time at my place.

After that, we took turns flying back and forth between Portland and Berkeley on a monthly basis. We met on the southern Oregon coast to introduce our dogs. To say it didn't go well is an understatement. Shortly after we had both arrived, Bart opened the gate to our weekend rental house, not realizing my dogs were inside the fenced-in yard. His seventy-five-pound white German shepherd, Sulay, surprised by seeing my dogs, went for McGee. One-third the shepherd's size, McGee snarled as loud as Sulay did, but was a wimp when it came to defending himself. In the fracas, Bart ended up with a bloody arm from falling on the gravel road where the dogs ran to continue their fighting. I was able to grab my puppy, but was bitten on my right hand when I tried to extract McGee's head from Sulay's mouth. It was not the successful introduction we'd anticipated, though the dogs emerged intact. No emergency vet visit was required. Only the humans bled. Bart's elbow became infected and remained so for two months.

In Portland, we managed to keep Sulay away from my smaller dogs with an extensive system of crates, portable gates, and moveable wire fences, along with constant surveillance. Bart built a corral in his backyard for my dogs to separate them from his dog and to ease the demand for early morning and late night walks in what Portlanders refer to as "drizzle," a weather condition a Californian would call "rain." We worked for months with one trainer who gave us little hope for a harmonious outcome, and then with a second trainer, Chris, whose star in the pantheon of dog trainers is well deserved. While our dogs never achieved a canine connection to mirror our human romance, it got increasingly tolerable.

In the meantime, everything else went easily, as if we had known one another for years, not months. We began cooking together. The man loves to eat and was accustomed to making his own meals, eating at the dinner table, and cleaning up after himself with ease. I gently forced my way into his kitchen, not wanting him to wait on me. If I asked where a pot or pan was or where a paring knife or colander could be found, he would retrieve it for me, rather than tell me where I could find it. "No,

Bart, sweetie, I want to know where it is, not have you give it to me" was my rote reaction to his gracious assistance, supplied multiple times a day.

We fell into a pattern where he would grill the meat, I would make the salad and a side dish—he especially liked a curried rice I make with thin slices of lemon, julienned red bell pepper, and chopped onions, garlic, and celery. We'd sit down together at the table, toast one another with a glass of wine, and sigh with wonder and disbelief. Was this really happening? Yes, it was.

I relished learning what foods he liked—deviled eggs are high on his list, and my deviled eggs are spectacular, if I do say so myself—and made extra chili, spaghetti, chicken cacciatore, and rice dishes to freeze for him to eat in my absence. He began introducing me to his friends, and we went out with them to lunch and invited them to dinner. But more than meals, I looked forward to our morning wake-ups. While Bart shaved with the radio on, I showered. To my delight, a slender arm made its way through the shower curtain, and a cup of coffee with milk appeared on the ledge next to the shampoo. After drying off, warmed by my first cup of shower-time coffee, I began putting his towel in the clothes dryer and handing it to him as he emerged seven minutes later. I looked forward to watching him rub a fluffy warm towel on his torso on chilly Oregon mornings.

We'd developed rituals, which triggered my memory of a remark he'd made in a phone call early on. "These days we're filling each other in about our pasts. We're letting each other know what we've been through, our history, good and bad, divorces and deaths. Soon we'll be done with that and start creating a present and a future." (Sweet Pea: "He was right on." Steve: "Yup.")

We'd been creating that present with every visit, trying to alter old habits established over decades with previous partners.

We shared our deepest thoughts and feelings for the first time since Patti's and Matt's deaths. For the most part, we laughed at each other's foibles. Bart complained I drove too cautiously. I thought he vacuumed the carpets too frequently and insisted he stop pressing his jeans. He couldn't believe I enjoyed drinking milk at lunchtime. I worried he sprinkled too much salt on his food—how could he taste his meat and potatoes? The list went on. The most off-the-wall feedback I got was when I asked him, "Is there anything I do that annoys you?" to which he responded, "Yes, but I don't want to tell you."

"Tell me," I insisted.

"You don't leave a tail on the toilet paper."

When we weren't together, Bart and I spoke every night at nine o'clock. We continued sharing the same mundane details about what we did at the gym, what we ate for lunch, what we were reading, and what movies and DVDs we'd watched. But we went deeper, talking about past career pressures and challenges, postretirement activities, days of eating alone and lonely sleepless nights, friends who'd hung in with us in the bleak times, and our uphill fight against inertia and aging. We talked about what angered us and what raised our spirits. We were corny—talking sunrises and sunsets and rain and rainbows. We ended our hour-long conversations with, "I love you."

The boy had learned to talk.

In no time we were visiting back and forth twice a month. Mostly I flew up to Portland because of the ease of my dog care arrangements. I had a dream tenant, Mary, who cared for McGee and Grace with such nurturing they didn't notice my absence. All they cared about was that nothing in their eating and sleeping schedules changed, plus they got more trips to the park and more opportunities for mountain hikes and beach runs.

Whenever time allowed, Bart flew down, and we drove up the magnificent Oregon Coast so my canine companions could be with us. And Bart and I would talk and talk. This quiet man stated matter-of-factly, "I've said more to you in a few months than I have total to everyone in the past ten years." I asked if he really meant everyone, or just to people at work. "No, everyone."

Bart's tales of his 1950s Southern boyhood enchanted me. When he was seven years old, his parents bought several dozen chickens, so the family could eat them fresh without having to go to the grocery store. His father brought the coops home at lunch time and then returned to work at the Dodge-Plymouth dealership he owned in Newton. Once they were alone, Bart persuaded younger brother Dickie to help him carry the coops inside and release the chickens. "We wanted to let them loose, so we could see what that looked like. Well, I wanted to, and Dickie went along with it." The chickens flapped, flew, and pooped in the kitchen, living room, and hallways. Fortunately the bedroom doors were closed. When his parents came home and viewed the mess created by the still-flapping, still-excreting chickens, Bart and brother Dickie were whipped with a belt. "But it was worth it," Bart drawled with a grin spreading across his face. "Sure, the whupping hurt plenty, but it only lasted five minutes. But more than sixty-five years later, I remember the fun of watching the chickens. It was definitely worth it."

When he wasn't shooting crawfish with his BB gun in a creek behind his house, making bows and arrows from chinaberry tree branches, or sucking honeysuckle and picking plums, he and his friends rode their bicycles to the railroad station to watch the trains go by. One time, his friend Jerry, pitcher on the little league team for which Bart played second base, stationed his bike in the road, leaving the kickstand down. Bart warned Jerry that, if he left his bike there, "I'll run into it." "No, you won't," his friend countered. "Yes, I will," was Bart's instant retort. "No, you won't." "Yes, I will." Bart pedaled as fast as he could and crashed dead-center into Jerry's bike. I asked if he'd damaged the bike, to which Bart replied, "Well, his bike was slightly dented, but Jerry bent it back into shape. I took the brunt of it—I was bleeding, scraped, and bruised. But I had to do it because he dared me. I pretty much always accepted dares."

The more stories Bart told, the more I learned that this courtly, logical, serious man had been a hellion. As early as first grade, his teachers had smacked his hands with a ruler for disobedient behavior. In junior high, his coach whacked him with a paddle with holes drilled in it. "He told us if we violated certain clearly established rules, that's what would happen, but I remember choosing to do it, intentionally crossing the line to test him. I remember how much the five gold-standard blows hurt. But I needed to see if he'd carry out his threat. My father said I deserved the punishment, and I agreed with him."

This straight A student continued his confrontations with authority in high school, causing two of his teachers to throw erasers at him in class. "I wanted them to know they were boring me or annoying me or whatever. In Spanish class I pretended to fall asleep. I was a wise-ass." He shook his head and added, "I don't know what was going on in my twisted mind, but I had to push the limits. I still do, just not in the same way."

I was eager for Bart to explain how the confrontational little boy had turned into the extraordinary human being he had become. Music had been a big part of it. I already knew he'd played alto sax in a rock band in high school in Meridian, the town of fifty thousand to which the family moved when his father bought a Chrysler–Plymouth dealership. Bart winced, remembering the band's first performance at the Meridian Teen Canteen. They'd sounded so bad that at intermission the kids turned on the juke box and told the band they wanted to keep it on. Bart and his pals, hurt and embarrassed, pushed their instruments out a window at the back of the large room while the crowd of teenagers kept dancing. Then, as unobtrusively as possible, they climbed out the window. "We thought, at least by our standards, that we sounded pretty good. But they didn't think so. Do you know how hard it is to push a drum set and an amplifier out a window without damaging them? And how humiliating it was to go to school on Monday morning?"

The group's musical talents improved, and they were never thrown out again. The band, known as the Lancers Seven, played at post-football parties and high school dances for forty dollars a night, split eight ways to include brother Dickie, who managed the band. In his junior and senior years, Bart was chosen drum major of the Meridian High School band. It placed first every year in the state competition and, in Bart's senior year, came in first in a tri-state competition. When I told Bart I couldn't imagine him high-stepping in a formfitting white silk suit with a feathered hat and moving a baton up and down to lead over a hundred musicians down a football field, he slow-talked his response, "I really liked it. I could lead, but didn't have to talk. That was the first time I realized I liked to lead."

In addition to music, cars played a big part in Bart's adolescence. He told me in detail about the 1951 gray-and-maroon Nash his father gave him for his fifteenth birthday, with the understanding that he agree to drive Dickie to and from school. "The heater didn't work and the windows didn't roll up all the way. When I was with a girl, I put newspaper at the top of the window, so we could stay warm as we kissed." (He was too polite to say, "made out" or "petted," though I knew that was what he meant.) "I carried oil and water with me because of leaks and wire for when the exhaust pipe fell off. And the transmission often got stuck in second gear." He was occasionally allowed to borrow his father's pink Chrysler New Yorker convertible. "It had a record player mounted under the dashboard, the only one I've ever seen. It played forty-five RPM records, one at a time. I could play Elvis, Chuck Berry, Jerry Lee Lewis—any record I wanted. All my friends wanted to ride with me when I could get that car."

I was especially interested in how Bart had decided to become a doctor. I've always had the idea that a person who's gone through the rigors of medical school to become a physician must have felt a profound calling, but that was not the case with Bart. For six months in high school, he wanted to be a Presbyterian minister. At age sixteen, he gave a sermon at his church on the subject of Jonah and the whale. "My sermon centered on the fact that we never know what we'll do under pressure, how we'll act under unforeseen circumstances. But the minister thing didn't last long. I knew myself well enough to know I didn't want to have to conform my behavior to other people's expectations. And there was another thing: I couldn't get satisfactory explanations regarding issues like predestination—that was a big one. I didn't buy it."

Next he considered being a nuclear physicist, without understanding what a nuclear physicist was. The summer before his senior year in high school, Bart received a National Science Foundation fellowship to attend an LSU program put on by scientists and engineers. "I enjoyed it, but it wasn't my thing. As far as the scientists went, I realized they were busy looking for grants and doing research I wasn't interested in. So I asked myself, 'What about being a doctor?' It would give me a reasonable amount of autonomy. And the freedom to decide where to live.

My economic needs could be met, but I didn't figure I'd make a big living. And I found I liked it. I really liked it."

He told me about a fellowship in Indianapolis after his second year of medical school; he spent the summer focusing on treatment of tuberculosis patients. The following summer he worked for three months with nondenominational Protestant missionaries in Manoram, a small village in Thailand. "I wanted to see how health care delivery worked in impoverished rural areas. I wanted to learn about the culture of a part of Southeast Asia, so different from what I was used to. If possible, I wanted to understand what was happening in Vietnam, though that didn't happen. Most of all, I wanted to experience a new way of thinking, living, and working. And even of eating. We ate rice and vegetables." And this from a man who loves bacon, steak, hot dogs, and hamburgers.

The all-time best story happened in his third year of medical school, when Bart was working at the Veterans Administration hospital in Jackson. He and his fellow med students were tending to an African-American patient who, to all appearances, was dying. This World War II vet was losing weight at a rapid pace. His vital signs were nosediving. He was "dwindling," a term doctors used when there was no diagnosable cause—no heart failure or pulmonary issues, no diabetes or cancer, no obvious explanation for his imminent mortality other than a failure to thrive. In the absence of medical evidence to assist with a diagnosis, Bart decided to ask the patient why he thought he was dying.

"'Cause Ah been hexed," was the moribund vet's answer. "Ahm gonna die 'cause a hex been placed on me. Ain't nothing you can do."

Unwilling to accept that death was inevitable, Bart recruited two fellow students to help him try to heal their charge.

"We had no idea how to unhex him," Bart explained to me. "There was no Internet back then to Google how to remove a death spell. So we did the best we could, making sure not to scare him." Around three o'clock the next morning, a time they figured no one would notice them, they went into his room. "We covered ourselves in sheets, held lighted candles in our hands, and hummed softly. We chanted just loud enough to wake him up. 'We are unhexing you. You are no longer hexed. You will live.' We made *ooh* and *ahh* sounds, along with the chanting."

As their patient gradually woke up, Bart and his pals continued moving slowly around his bed, waving the candles over his head and body, chanting reassuringly. The following day the patient began eating. Within a week he was discharged. His recovery was determined to be a medical miracle.

When I asked Bart if he and his friends had told the supervising doctor what they had done, he scoffed, "Of course not. He'd have thought we were crazy. We would have been reprimanded. But it worked. We had nothing to lose and everything to gain. That's the problem with some doctors—they don't think to ask the patient what's wrong. They think they know. You need to involve the patient."

In the middle of the hot, humid summer, we met in New Orleans, and I introduced him to my girlfriends and neighbors, who overwhelmingly approved of this new man in my life. We rented a car and drove to his hometown of Newton, Mississippi, with its population of thirty-five hundred and one traffic light. We continued on to Meridian, where he went to junior high school and high school. The high point of the trip was meeting Bart's spritely, diminutive ninety-year-old Aunt Doris in Jackson. She greeted me with, "Ah'm glad to meet you. Do you love mah sweet boy?" I assured her I did.

"Does he love you?" she inquired.

"Aunt Doris, you'll have to ask him."

"No need," she assured me. "Ah think he does."

The more I fell in love with Bart, the more it struck me how dissimilar Bart and Matt were physically, culturally, and temperamentally. Bart was tall, slender, light-skinned, and light-haired, with blue eyes. Matt was a good three inches shorter, olive-skinned, with balding brown hair and brown eyes. He had the build of a wrestler or a boxer, while Bart reminded me of a lithe, athletic Greek youth pictured on a vase or mosaic in a museum. Matt loved to perform. Bart avoided the limelight. He liked being the backup man in the band.

And yet my reaction to my first encounter with each of them was similar to the point of being scary. Within less than an hour of meeting them, I was transported to a place in my heart that had not been filled by any man other than these two: one, a boisterous, street-smart Jewish lawyer from multiethnic Brooklyn and the other, a soft-talking, courtly, WASPy Southerner from a small Mississippi town. I felt the same heart palpitations within a ridiculously short period and yearned for a deep connection that would endure over as long a time as life would afford us.

Maybe that connection started because of their basic similarities. Both were intelligent, with a deep intellectual hunger, self-confidence, and a well-developed politically liberal credo. Both were committed to an energetic, fit life; both liked and had dogs. Equally critical, both men shopped, cooked, cleaned, and vacuumed, and they liked sharing that role with a partner.

But they looked, talked, and behaved so differently.

One huge difference between the two of them was their feelings about children. Matt had stayed in his marriage seven years too long because he couldn't imagine leaving his four daughters. He'd loved being a father; he was fierce about his girls. I thought of this highly masculine man as a ferocious mama bear. And I'd always wanted to have children, ideally two or three.

When I asked Bart why he and his first wife hadn't had children, he explained, "Early on, I assumed we'd have a family, but I got more and more into my career. And Susan didn't want to have a child. If she had, I'd have been fine with it." After they were divorced, and he remarried, he helped raise his stepdaughter, Amy. "And Patti had had a hysterectomy. So that was that. I don't feel I've missed out on anything."

At seventy-four, though there was no point in revisiting his decision, I still wanted to know if he liked kids and if he missed having grandchildren. I wondered, "Bart, if I had met you earlier, in my thirties, I would have wanted another child. Would that have been all right?"

His response was both sweet and unusual. "I do like kids, but not like you do. If we'd been together then, and having a family was important to you, we'd have done whatever you wanted." He went on to say, "But there's another thing, and I know it will sound strange. I wouldn't want a child to go through what I went through. I wasn't easy. I don't know why I was the way I was. My parents could have killed me, and no one would have blamed them. And yet I wouldn't have wanted a child who wasn't like me."

I wondered if their differences made it easy for me to love Bart and no longer miss Matt. One was not more or less than the other. Bart was an unparalleled version of Bart. Or maybe it was the two versions of me—the thirty-four-year-old divorced mother struggling to support herself and her young daughter, and the seventy-four-year-old retired widow—responding to each man. But ultimately it didn't matter. I was completely in love with Bart.

A year after we met, Bart and I drove down to Palm Desert, where he had arranged a five-day house swap with a friend. On the day before Valentine's Day and two days before my birthday, we spent the day at the Palm Springs Aerial Tramway, the world's largest rotating tramway, with a panoramic view of Chino Canyon and Mt. San Jacinto State Park. The views had been disappointing, with rain and mist obscuring visibility. Afterward, we drove to John Henry's Café for a six o'clock dinner. We asked to be seated in the outdoor patio under an umbrella sheltering us from the fine drizzle, with a propane heater nearby and a vine-covered stucco wall across from our table.

It was dusk as we ordered cocktails. We felt cozy and coddled by the harmonious surroundings and friendly waitstaff. We held hands. Dusk gave way to evening darkness, but the lights from inside the restaurant, the string lights sparkling on the patio, and the candle on our table made it easy to see each other. With no lead-in, apropos of nothing we'd been discussing, Bart looked at me and asked, "Do you think we should get married?"

My girlfriends had been telling me for several months they expected Bart was going to ask me to marry him, and I invariably shrugged. "No, he won't. There's no reason to." I had my justifications, "We're not going to have kids. We don't need the other's health insurance. We're both financially stable. Yes, I love him. Absolutely. But we're good. Why mess with a good thing?" When one girlfriend had even suggested I propose to him, I was resolute. "I'm not going to propose to any man. We might end up living together, but not get married. I don't want to unless for whatever reason it's important to him, then I'll say yes—but will insist we wait a while." I knew my mind.

I was pretty sure I'd heard him correctly, but he might as well have been asking, "Would you like some bread?" It certainly wasn't my idea of a proper marriage proposal. But he had made himself very clear. I looked at the face I had quickly grown to cherish. I did not hesitate. I had no preconditions.

I said, "Yes."

(And Sweet Pea and Steve were speechless.)

EPILOGUE

"LOUISIANA WOMAN, MISSISSIPPI MAN"

(Loretta Lynn and Conway Twitty)

We drove home from John Henry's mist-graced café, my hand on Bart's right leg, as is my custom when he is at the wheel. We hardly spoke. From time to time he stroked my hand. I continued to be amazed by his seven-word question and my one-word response that had altered our present and future. Within half an hour, we were brushing and flossing and getting out of our day clothes and into bed. Usually at this point in the evening we spoke about the day's doings and what we might do the next day, but we didn't that night. We just went to bed, knowing we'd made a significant decision.

The next morning, Valentine's Day, I wondered if he'd spoken prematurely and asked, "Do you want to think about this more?"

"No, I don't," he said. "I'm sure."

The following day, my birthday, I asked yet again, "Are you sure you want to do this?"

"Yes, I do."

I questioned him four times, each time as we woke up, and each time he answered me with an assured I-want-to-marry-you response. After the fourth time, I said, "Okay then. I guess we're doing this," but I added that the proposal seemed to have come out of the blue.

"No, I've been thinking about it for at least three months, maybe more. I knew it was the right thing. But I didn't plan to ask you when I did. It just came out."

I was sure I loved Bart, but wanted to know what marriage meant at this point in our lives.

"Bart, what will change? I'm not going to leave Berkeley. We can go back and forth, and I'm happy to be in Portland more than you'll be in Berkeley. But I'm not selling my house or leaving my friends for good. Why are we doing this?"

My heart, already melted, melted more when he said, "Nothing will change. We'll be putting an exclamation point on what we already have." But the exclamation point led to another question mark when he asked, "When?"

I hadn't expected that question either, certainly not so soon, but apparently Bart was not one to dawdle when he'd made up his mind. We contacted Marcia and Herb to find out their schedule. We wanted Herb to get a Universal Life Church license and officiate as an ordained minister. When he agreed to conduct our ceremony, Marcia informed us she would be our flower girl. I wanted to give my sister time to fly back from a business trip in Tokyo and to invite my dear forever-friend Murray to come from New Orleans. She had been my "best rep" when I married Matt in our backyard in Berkeley, and she and her companion,

Harry, needed to be there. The presence of Bart's stepdaughter, Amy, and her husband, Kris, from Portland was mandatory, as was the presence of Bart's best friend, Bill, from high school and college in Mississippi and his wife, Sally.

On April 4, 2019, six weeks after Bart's proposal, in the late afternoon, we assembled for the ceremony in a private room at Restaurant La Gare, a French restaurant in historic Railroad Square in Santa Rosa. The rain that had been predicted for the past several days held off. I was a scarlet bride, wearing a red dress I found on sale (fifty percent off, with an additional thirty percent discount) at the Portland Airport branch of the women's clothing store McKenzie's. The mid-length dress had a scooped neck, a fitted bodice, a flowing gauzy overskirt, and a silky underskirt. Even though bright red for a wedding seemed a little excessive, I tried it on and loved it, as did Bart when I FaceTimed him from the airport to get his reaction. "But what will I wear?" was his concern. He wore a dapper gray suit and a dark red shirt, but I wouldn't let him wear a tie.

We concocted a trifecta of wedding favors for our guests. At my request, Amy and Kris burned CDs with a playlist of favorite songs, including those we'd emailed each other in our e-courting days. We added a few new ones: "Holly Holy" by Neil Diamond, "My Girl" by The Temptations, "Over the Rainbow" by Israel (IZ) Kamakawiwo'ole, and "Only You" by The Platters. I wish I had added the most worthy and beautiful "There's Always One More Time" by Johnny Adams, a major oversight on my part.

The lead song on the CD for our friends was "Louisiana Woman, Mississippi Man" by Conway Twitty and Loretta Lynn. Some months before the wedding, when we were having breakfast at the Waffle House (Bart loves a good Waffle House) in Slidell, Louisiana, a customer heard me talking with our waitress.

She had asked where we had driven from (New Orleans) and where we were heading (Newton, with its chicken coop history, Meridian, and Jackson). When she asked why we'd chosen those destinations, I said, "Because I'm from Louisiana and he's from Mississippi. We're going to see the places where he grew up and visit with his aunt in Jackson." At that, the customer in the booth next to ours stood up and broke into song, describing how much a Looziana woman and a M'ssippi man loved one another; how the mighty river couldn't keep them apart because there was too much love in each person's heart; and how he jumped into the river and outswam the 'gators to reach his beloved on the other side of the Big Muddy. That clinched it. We had our theme song and ordered Waffle House mugs as an additional wedding favor to accompany the CDs.

A final gift was friendship quotes I glued on popsicle sticks, written in Waffle House colors of black and yellow, to insert into the mugs. For dear best rep, Murray, an avid gardener, I had Proust's words, "Friends are gardeners who plant flowers in our souls."

Hubert Humphrey's quote was for my sister, Virginia: "The greatest gift of life is friendship, and I have received it." Other quotes included: "There is nothing on this earth more to be prized than friendship" (Thomas Aquinas), "Friendship is a sheltering tree" (Samuel Taylor Coleridge), and "A friend may well be reckoned the masterpiece of nature" (Ralph Waldo Emerson). For Bart I quoted: "Love is friendship set to music," variously attributed to Channing Pollock, Joseph Campbell, and Jackson Pollock.

Officiant Herb took his role seriously, calling us several times to help with the plans for the ceremony. Love Liaison Marcia kept telling me I should be taking our wedding preparations more seriously at the same time she was insisting on being our flower girl. She bought an Easter basket for the red rose petals she would strew at the feet of everyone in the room. "Here I, who take my Jewish faith seriously, went and bought a Christian basket," she chuckled. Herb played the ukulele, and Marcia led the singing to "Always" by Irving Berlin and "Annie's Song" by John Denver. Murray read an e.e. cummings poem that I didn't know, "i carry your heart with me (i carry it in my heart)," that made me cry. Bill followed Murray, and, among other things, quoted snippets from Robert Fulghum's *True Love*, prompting both laughter and tears.

Bart choked up as he delivered his remarks, thanking Bill, Amy, and Marcia for staying in touch during the hard times and helping him "keep my head on straight and finding a new way for the last two years." He ended his comments to them saying, "I am grateful to you in ways you can never know." He continued, "Sallie and I found ourselves talking on the phone day and night. Long talks. Those of you who know me, know I don't talk very much. But that changed." Turning to me, he concluded, "I have found a new world; that world is with Sallie. I commit to being your partner. To loving you. To being present for you, wherever that takes us."

I spoke next, holding tight to Murray's hand as I read my piece, my eyes watering, blurring the text. It hadn't occurred to me I'd be teary, much less in full-cry mode. There were no napkins in sight and I didn't have a tissue, so I grabbed a folded tablecloth from a serving table to wipe my untidy nose. I talked about the role music had played in our evening conversations, as we grew closer in the weeks of communicating by phone and the computer. I recounted the titles of songs we'd exchanged, songs we'd played before the ceremony and had included on the CDs we had given everyone. Still holding on to Murray's hand and facing Bart, I committed to making him sugar cookies, deviled eggs, and popcorn, to loving, respecting, honoring, caring for, and supporting him, but not to obeying him.

It was a day of grace and of lightness for "a Looziana woman and a M'ssippi man." It was a day of joy overcoming loss, of serendipity and concerted effort on the part of family (my sister and nephew of the PASTRAMI Advisory Committee) and friends (Marcia and Herb) to bring us to this day.

We served popcorn and champagne, danced to our playlist, and then had a French-accented dinner, ample bottles of wine and Perrier, and a loving roast, in which our guests got to recount embarrassing stories from yesteryear about the bride and groom.

After dinner, everyone left with their wedding favors and their copy of the pink wedding program, decorated with magnolias, the official flower of both our home states. On the back of the program, Bart and I had printed a "Heartfelt Acknowledgements" section that read:

We are touched that you are celebrating with us today.
Thank you for sharing in our act of commitment.

Words fail to express our gratitude to Marcia and Dr. Herbie Pie for bringing us together. Without Marcia's introduction, we would not be leaping head- and heart-first into these sparkling marital waters.

We remember with deepest affection those we have long loved and continue to love. We carry Patti and Matt in our hearts.

For months before Bart asked me to marry him, I'd been begging Marcia to let me tell about PASTRAMI, so I could come clean about how we had steered him into my sights. She refused, saying he'd be angry with her if he learned of our conspiracy. She was certain he would have refused her efforts to lure him out of his grief. But all along he'd been telling me he knew what she had done. "I was sure she set us up. But I trusted her taste—if she wanted to introduce me to someone she thought I would like, I wanted to meet her. And that would be *you*."

Invariably I said, "Yes, she did knowingly introduce us. She knew I was actively looking and told me I would like you, but she had no way of knowing whether we'd fall for one another." But I wanted to spill all the beans and say, "Bart, I approached her about introducing me to a likely soul mate. I had a website and asked her to look at it. She did. And I am and will always be eternally grateful to her." Friends who knew about my project pushed me to ignore my promise to Marcia and tell Bart, but I couldn't. My sister volunteered to mention PASTRAMI to Bart "accidentally on purpose," to relieve me of feeling I had lied to him by omission.

The morning after our wedding, the matter was resolved without any devious action on my part. Bart had been cleaning my car for our drive back to Portland and had rifled through the glove compartment to make sure the car registration and insurance papers were there. My sister and I were sitting on the living room sofa when Bart walked in the front door. He had a quizzical look on his face and an array of bright orange, hot pink, and lime green cards and envelopes in his hands—they were the PASTRAMI handouts I had left there. I'd forgotten about them ever since meeting Bart.

"What's this?" he inquired, holding up the colorful papers. Virginia and I burst into sisterly gales of laughter. I hadn't broken my promise after all and didn't need to worry anymore. Marcia couldn't fault me for having my search-for-a-soul-mate handouts in a private place, gathering dust alongside the window ice-scraper, flashlight, and assorted road maps.

Bart was equally delighted, announcing jubilantly, "I was right! I knew all along she was up to something." He wasn't angry or the slightest bit annoyed. I handed him an overstuffed manila folder with a hard copy of the text and images from the dismantled PASTRAMI site. Bart studied every letter of "PASTRAMI, ETC," looked at the descriptions under each letter, and drawled, "But I don't measure up to this."

"Oh, Bart, yes, you do."

I had to remind Marcia more than once of the five-thousand-dollar finder's fee. For weeks she refused to comply with my request to give me her list of charitable organizations, insisting, "I didn't do it for the money." I persisted and, in time, she gave in. Over the summer I made contributions to her designated 501(c)(3)s: Planned Parenthood; climate advocate 350 Bay Area; Compassion and Choices, provider of care and choice in end-of-life cases; San Diego Emergency Response, an organization that assists immigrants at the border; Interfaith Movement for Human Integrity, which mobilizes congregations to take stands on social justice issues; and finally Crisis Nursery, an agency that helps prevent child abuse. A citizen-activist with energy to spare, Marcia volunteers with many of these organizations and cares deeply about the issues she champions. Each time I wrote a check, it felt like Christmas.

Since we got married, Bart and I have been going back and forth between our cities, sometimes flying and dog-less, sometimes driving and dog-accompanied, with me being in Portland more than in California. Bart comes to the Bay Area whenever we drive and stays in Berkeley for short spurts. On every trip, we have dinner with at least one or more of my girlfriends and couple friends. During the one-quarter of the time we spend apart, we have short phone chats from early morning to late afternoon, followed by a longer conversation at bedtime. We text and email intermittently, though the practice of sending song titles has ended. We listen to music together now.

Life with luminous Bart is markedly different from my twenty-four-year life with technicolor Matt. We're older by decades and mellower, though both of us are filled with energy. We're making his house ours, turning his life and my life into our life, and forging new connections in Portland. My efforts at making new friends aren't progressing as quickly as I'd like. I want girlfriends to walk, talk, and have coffee with; I'm eager to join a reading group. I deeply miss my longtime Berkeley pals, Berkeley Rotary activities and friendships, and volunteer commitments and connections. A fish out of the Bay Area waters where I've spent over four decades, I am learning to navigate Portland—its streets, neighborhoods, waterfront area, and numerous bridges, parks, and hiking paths, not to mention its medical offices, coffee shops, and grocery stores. Now I have a second home base. From our bedroom, we watch the sun rise in the morning over a backyard rich in ferns, rhododendrons, rose bushes, hinoki cypress, and towering redwoods. And the fiddleberries of all sizes and shapes—that's what Bart calls the plants and trees whose names he doesn't know.

However much we have marveled at our new lease on life, we have not been spared its complications. The dog conflict was the easier part, although it hasn't gotten what I would call easy to keep Bart's German shepherd away from wimpy McGee, who won't defend himself. Health issues have cut deeper. Marcia had told me before I met him that Bart had slow-growing prostate cancer, but she didn't mention that he'd rejected recommended radiation treatment. When I learned of his intention not to pursue medical intervention, he said, "All I wanted was to live one day after the dog died. Then I met you, and that has changed my decision and my life." I was with him in Portland for over half of his thirty-nine treatments.

After we got married, and the results of his check-ups were encouraging, more medical problems surfaced. Bart told me he was experiencing anomalies in his throat and upper esophagus when he ate. He consulted with a gastroenterologist, an ENT doctor, and a radiologist. He had a biopsy done of his upper esophagus. I was terrified to hear the word "esophageal" connected with Bart. Ultimately all results were negative, with a diagnosis of age-related swallowing difficulties that were completely manageable. A follow-up speech therapy consultation pointed out the need for him to modify a few habits: Bart should eat slowly, not talk and eat at the same time, and refrain from eating crackers (or his beloved popcorn or nuts) while lying down. And, fortunately, his impaired peristaltic action did not affect his kissing capabilities.

At the same time he was undergoing his medical adventures, I, who had been healthy for my entire life, began having short episodes of numbness on the right side of my mouth and in my right arm and occasional longer spells where I couldn't stand or sit up without toppling over. Over a two-month period, I experienced four to eight "waves" a day, usually of short duration, with a rare one lasting up to half an hour and even longer. On Heather's birthday, I had seventeen waves; one of them continued for over an hour. Bart, ever the medical practitioner with a bedside manner more clinical than romantic, took my blood pressure and pulse every day, usually multiple times. He looked for evidence to suggest I might be experiencing cognitive impairment, transient ischemic attacks, or neurologic migraines. The pattern of my symptoms didn't fit any of those categories. At the onset of the seizures, he had rushed me to the emergency room. Several weeks later, he had to drag my limp body to the car for a scheduled MRI. The ultimate neurological diagnosis was sensory seizures, caused by electrical brain wiring gone haywire, most assuredly triggered by individual episodes of anxiety and stress, and corrected by medication with no side effects. Bart and I have established another ritual: taking care of one another under adverse circumstances.

As I end this book, I am struck—as I have been over and over throughout my seventy-five years—at the role chance plays in our lives. It was chance that brought Matt and me together. Four decades later, it was chance that Marcia and I met in Cuba, lived within a half-hour's drive of each other and, most notably, forged a deeper relationship once we returned to our homes. It was chance that I met Shelley vacuuming her car on the street and chance that her husband had known Bart years earlier. Their enthusiasm for Bart and me as a potential couple made me think there might be a needle in the haystack after all.

I once said to Bart, "It's amazing that we get along as well as we do, at our age, and with our different life experiences and ingrained habits."

He took issue with my statement. "No, it's not amazing that we get along so well. I knew we would when I met you. What's amazing is that we met at all. After that, it was easy and natural."

Thank you, Marcia. Thank you, Gin and Clayton. Thank you, Universe.

APPLAUSE GOES TO . . .

(otherwise known as
the ACKNOWLEDGMENTS section)

It is daunting to acknowledge those who have helped my memoir come to published life. I don't want to leave out a single person who has helped me get to this point in this narrative and, to a great extent, to this point in my life. I know there'll be someone I neglect to mention. Whoever you are, please forgive me.

My first round of applause goes to Jane Staw. When I asked Jane, a Berkeley-based published writer and professional writing coach, to help me tell my story, she became my confidante and, unexpectedly, my social worker. Jane extracted memories I had chosen to bury, some consciously and some unconsciously. She pushed gently, but insistently, for subcutaneous excavation, encouraging me to dig deeper and write deeper. She made me venture into the dark holes. At the time I had no idea where the book was going or if it was going anywhere. Jane said we'd figure it out. She was right, of course.

Once Jane and her husband, Steve, left the country for a few months, I approached longtime friend Courtney Flavin to help edit the chapters I'd written under Jane's tutelage. Our personal connection goes back more than forty-five years, to when I was a single mother. Courtney helped me organize the book and recalled anecdotes and memories I'd neglected to insert in earlier chapters. She insisted on finding the humor in some of my misadventures. Without Courtney's "funny red pen," this book and my life would be much less rich.

Virginia Littlejohn played multiple roles, as supportive sister, managing editor of the PASTRAMI website, and captain of the PASTRAMI cheerleading team, with my nephew Clayton Littlejohn Johnson as graphic designer, webmaster, and cheerleader. Not only did Virginia stay in touch when she sensed my energy flagging, she also read chapters of this book a number of times. She pushed me, as did Jane and Courtney, to include unsettling memories, as well as hilarious ones. Thank you, Gin and Clayton. We'll always have the Failed Candidate, won't we?

Invaluable collaborators who provided input in the early days of structuring the PASTRAMI project include my stepdaughter Beth Haiken and her husband, Steve Aibel; my should-have-been daughter, Tracy Sullivan; and prized Berkeley Rotarian friends Tina Etcheverry and Shawn Rowles. I want to acknowledge the efforts of Love Liaisons who helped move my search forward: Berkeley Rotarians Shawn (again), Jim Masters, John Ferguson, and Judith Glass; my Spanish student of fifteen years, Caroline Peterson; and, of course, Marcia Liberson and her husband, Herb Salomon. On the writing side of all this, Berkeley Rotarians Pate Thompson, Peter Campbell, and Jim Masters provided input for several chapters, including sailing terms. Stepdaughter Claire shared with me her memory of the morning Matt died, a luminous episode I hadn't heard before. And I can't forget wise Theo in Peru and life coach Bill Say in Berkeley. They guided my steps.

Cherished readers, whose comments, constructive criticism, and "atta-girl" compliments kept me moving forward include Dave and Genie Killoran, Beth Haiken, Kate Sutliff, and Marilee Eaves. And then there's Murray Pitts, whom I've known longer than I've known anyone but my sister. Murray read and made welcome suggestions. She was my best rep for my marriages to Matt and Bart, four decades apart. Her hand is the one I grasp on good days and sad ones.

Finally, I want to applaud the She Writes Press professionals who assisted me in putting this book out into the world. In addition, peerless info-sleuth Barrett Briske and incomparable publicist Caitlin Hamilton generously pointed the way whenever I turned to them for help and direction.

All these people and more stand tall in my heart, like redwoods in the Peace Grove at Tilden Park. Thank you. Deepest thanks, y'all.

BOOK CLUB GUIDE

1. Does this book make you think differently about dating late in life?
2. Have you tried different dating websites and groups? Was your experience similar to Sallie's?
3. How does this memoir make you view retirement? Does it change how you view aging?
4. What anchors sustained Sallie through her grief? What sustained her in her search for love?
5. There is a theme in this memoir of helping others and also of asking for help. Discuss.
6. How does Sallie define family in this memoir?
7. Discuss the importance of place and of home in this book.
8. In this memoir, there are moments Sallie must be brave. How and when are we brave in our lives?
9. *Yes, Again* is about the importance of connecting with others. Is it also about connecting with ourselves? Discuss.

ABOUT THE AUTHOR

SALLIE H. WEISSINGER is a native of New Orleans and was raised as a military brat away from the South (Germany, New Mexico, Ohio, Japan, and Michigan). Every summer, she and her family returned to visit her mother's relatives in New Orleans and her father's family in a small Alabama town. She has lived most of her life in the Bay Area and also in New Orleans. These days, "home" includes not only New Orleans and Berkeley, but also Portland, Oregon, where she lives most of the time with her husband, Bart McMullan, a retired internal medicine doctor and health care executive, and their three dogs. A retired executive herself, she now teaches Spanish and does medical interpreting for non-profit organizations in Central America and the Dominican Republic. Weissinger is a passionate member of the Berkeley Rotary Club and has served on the boards of Berkeley Rotary, the Aurora Theatre in Berkeley, and the East Bay (formerly Oakland) SPCA. Find her online at www.yesagainmemoir.com.

Selected Titles from She Writes Press

She Writes Press is an independent publishing company founded to serve women writers everywhere. Visit us at www.shewritespress.com.

Miracle at Midlife: A Transatlantic Romance by Roni Beth Tower. $16.95, 978-1-63152-123-2. An inspiring memoir chronicling the sudden, unexpected, and life-changing two-year courtship between a divorced American lawyer living on a houseboat in the center of Paris and an empty-nested clinical psychologist living in Connecticut.

The Buddha at My Table: How I Found Peace in Betrayal and Divorce by Tammy Letherer. $16.95, On a Tuesday night, just before Christmas, after he had put their three children in bed, Tammy Letherer's husband shattered her world and destroyed every assumption she'd ever made about love, friendship, and faithfulness. In the aftermath of this betrayal, however, she finds unexpected blessings—and, ultimately, the path to freedom.

Splitting the Difference: A Heart-Shaped Memoir by Tré Miller-Rodríguez. $19.95, 978-1-938314-20-9. When 34-year-old Tré Miller-Rodríguez's husband dies suddenly from a heart attack, her grief sends her on an unexpected journey that culminates in a reunion with the biological daughter she gave up at 18.

Insatiable: A Memoir of Love Addiction by Shary Hauer. $16.95, 978-1-63152-982-5. An intimate and illuminating account of corporate executive—and secret love addict—Shary Hauer's migration from destructive to healthy love.

First Date Stories: Women's Romantic to Ridiculous Midlife Adventures by Jodi Klein. $16.95, 978-1-64742-185-4. A collection of hopeful, hilarious, and horrific tales—plus dating tips and inspirational quotes—designed to remind women in their mid-thirties and beyond that not all first dates are created equal, and sometimes they can be the beginning of something wonderful.

Big Wild Love: The Unstoppable Power of Letting Go by Jill Sherer Murray. $16.95, 978-1-63152-852-1. After staying in a dead-end relationship for twelve years, Jill Sherer Murray finally let go—and ultimately attracted the love she wanted. Here, she shares how, along with a process to help readers get unstuck and find their own big, wild love.